THE
VOICE
WITHIN

Long loved and cherished by the people shall I be
Because my lyre in hearts did kindness wake
And in this cruel age sing praise of liberty
And for the fallen plea of mercy make

Alexander Pushkin 1836
From **Exegi monumentum**
translated by Robert Daglish

ILLUSTRATED BY ALISON PRINCE

THE
VOICE
WITHIN

● ● ●

WINNING ENTRIES FROM
SCOTLAND AND RUSSIA
1989 TO 1998

The Pushkin Prizes in Scotland

The Pushkin Prizes in Scotland 1999

> The publication of this
> anthology has been made
> possible with the help of
> a generous grant from
> the Kintore Trust

Every effort has been made to contact the authors of all the pieces
in this anthology, for permission to reprint their work. In a few cases,
however, and for various reasons, this has not been possible.
We hope that the former pupils concerned will take this note as due
acknowledgment of their copyright, with our thanks to them,
and to all the other authors.

The Pushkin Prizes in Scotland
18 Crown Terrace
Glasgow G12 9ES
Tel & Fax: 0141-357 0327

ISBN 0 9534596 0 8

Accepted by the Inland Revenue as a
Charitable Trust (Ref. no. ED502/92/MEB)

Contents

Acknowledgments

We owe a great debt of gratitude to many people for the publication of this anthology. First of all our warmest thanks go to the Kintore Trust, whose very generous grant has enabled us to finance this project.

Then we would like to thank Professor Edwin Morgan, one of our first judges, for his inspiring introduction; and Alison Prince, the current Chair of the judges, not only for that role, but also for her charming illustrations and attractive cover design. We are grateful to Martin Dewhirst of the University of Glasgow, for help in the typing of the Russian version of *Auld Lang Syne*.

Members of our Executive Committee who formed the editorial committee and who have devoted much time and thought to the project were Lindsey Fraser, Executive Director of Scottish Book Trust; Maggie Corr, Strategic Library Services Manager, Edinburgh City Libraries; Valerie Bierman, Assistant Co-ordinator of our Russian section; and Mary Baxter, Co-ordinator of the Pushkin Prizes in Scotland, who has had the enormous task of overseeing the whole project.

Our trustees and other members of our Executive Committee have given us the benefit of much good advice; and we are also extremely grateful to all our judges, past and present, for the care with which they considered the hundreds of entries they read. In addition to those already mentioned, we are honoured to have had among them Norman MacCaig, Mollie Hunter, Joan Lingard, Magnus Linklater, Willis Pickard, Professor Douglas Dunn, Dilys Rose, Anne Fine, Professor Terry Wade, Iain Crichton Smith, Professor Roderick Watson, Meg Bateman and Ron Butlin.

Throughout the years we have been most appreciative of all the help and support we have received from Local Authority Directors of Education and their staff, together with the enthusiasm and commitment of the many teachers and children concerned, as well as the interest of the parents.

We also owe a great debt of gratitude to the team of Russian judges, led by their Chairman Vladimir Marantsman, and most of all to our Co-ordinator in St Petersburg, Natalia Ushmanova, whose dedication in promoting the Pushkin Prizes in the English-speaking schools in that city has been quite exceptional over these past testing years. We would like to record, too, our grateful thanks to Irene Dunlop, our Russian-speaking escort, for looking after our prizewinners so faithfully; to Elena Kotschutskaya for guiding them so brilliantly round St Petersburg; and for the ever-willing assistance and interest we have received from the Consulate of the Russian Federation in Edinburgh.

Finally, we would also like once more to take this opportunity of thanking all our sponsors and donors, past and present, whose support, particularly in the early years, has helped to keep the Pushkin Prizes in Scotland alive and growing.

Foreword

This anthology celebrates both the tenth year of the Pushkin Prizes in Scotland and the Bicentenary of Alexander Pushkin's birth in June 1799. It contains a cross-section of award-winning entries, not only from Scottish schools but also from some of the 35 English-speaking schools in St Petersburg.

What a host of talent has burst forth! A veritable treasure chest of imagination, emotions, wit, pathos and humour are all there to share, to marvel at and to enjoy. Little did I think that this simple scheme for secondary school pupils in their first two years, begun in a small way in Tayside Region, would spread the length and breadth of Scotland; its only object then, as now, to encourage and enable young people to dig deep and find their inner voice, and then enjoy the freedom of expressing it.

Alexander Pushkin continues to be the most loved poet and writer in Russia, a guiding light and uniting force. I feel it a great privilege as his great-great-granddaughter to have been able to help keep the flame of his creativity alight within today's young people of both countries, not only through their writing but also by providing the opportunity for them to meet and forge links of friendship and understanding.

Some of our participants have continued to write in the course of their careers. One works in journalism, another in radio. The poem of another was recently included in an anthology of poems, one for each day of the year. Many may never write anything else: the important thing is that they had a go, and that quite a number who had no success in their first year tried again and achieved a place on the Awards list at their second attempt.

So I have just one piece of advice to all the young people who read this anthology: never, ever give up! You all have a hidden talent. To find it, just pause and listen to The Voice Within.

Myra Butter

LADY BUTTER CVO, CHAIRMAN OF THE PUSHKIN PRIZES IN SCOTLAND

Editorial

The work in this anthology represents eight years of the Pushkin Prizes in Scotland. Inevitably, difficult choices had to be made, but the aim of the editorial team was to make this selection of forty-seven Prizewinning, Highly Commended and Commended entries as representative as possible of the thoughts and interests of the contributors, all pupils in the first two years of secondary school, that is, in the age range 12 to 14.

So as to include as many pieces as possible, only an extract of some of the longer stories is given. Others have been slightly shortened. The range is quite remarkable: it's not often, all in one book, that you can find a philosophical conversation with a dog, a letter from a Spanish parrot, an account of a Cossack weekend, a journey on a ghost train, poems on loneliness, fear, bullying, cats big and small, wild horses, a story about false teeth, thoughts on football, the tragedy of the *Iolaire*, and many more.

The St Petersburg scholars (age range 14 to 16) have to translate their work into English - not an easy task, from a language with no definite or indefinite article, and no use of the verb 'to be'. The many English tenses are an added complication; but shining through all their entries are a quality of imagination and a maturity of thought which deserve our admiration and respect.

It was decided to exclude any explanatory notes, comments and photographs; and to let the writing of the young authors stand on its own, enhanced only by Alison Prince's wonderfully sympathetic illustrations. It is a record of undiluted creativity, a book to amuse, to move, to learn from, but most of all, for everyone simply to enjoy.

Mary Baxter

MARY BAXTER
FOR EDITORIAL COMMITTEE

Introduction

It has been a great pleasure for me, over the years, to have some involvement with the Pushkin Prizes, which began enthusiastically but tentatively, and have now amply proved their worth. The present anthology will show how well justified the initiators of the project were, in their belief that Russia's national poet had something to say to us, and that his life and works and ideas and feelings could spark off new writing by students at Scottish schools.

The prizewinning contributions gathered here, from both Scottish and Russian students, have a wonderful variety and range. Some of the themes are what one would expect to find: schools and teachers, parents and children, old age and youth, contrasts between urban and rural life. But the net is cast much wider: Highland Clearances and Russian Cossacks, parrots and pigs, football and God, Nazis and Jews prisons and crop circles, a trip to the Sahara, and (not least) a retelling of Tam o Shanter from the young witch's point of view.

The impression one gains is that the Pushkin Prizes have encouraged young people in Scotland and Russia to take pleasure in the creative act of writing, to learn how to overcome the difficulties of casting out on your own and saying just what you want to say, and above all to exercise the imagination, as Pushkin did in his all too brief existence. The international aspect of the project is itself worth emphasising, particularly since the organising of visits from one country to another, with all their contacts, friendships, discoveries, surprises, and one might say revelations. The much-travelled Pushkin would certainly have said, Carry on: horses harnessed, rugs on the sleigh, and away!

EDWIN MORGAN

Preface

It was with some trepidation, ten years ago, that I and my colleagues in the Education Department of what was then Tayside Region greeted Lady Butter's proposal of a creative writing competition for secondary school pupils, to be linked with the name of the Russian writer Alexander Pushkin, a family connection.

Lady Butter had (and still has!) a great ability to pass on her enthusiasm and commitment to other people. I can well recall sitting with her at a meeting of Principal Teachers of English and being amazed at the ease with which she convinced them of the value to pupils of participating in such a competition.

It has been of great interest and satisfaction to observe the way in which the Pushkin Prizes project has developed over the years. Following the initial involvement of schools in Tayside, other authorities became interested, until now the competition can be accessed by pupils in all education authorities in Scotland.

Another pleasing feature of the competition has been the way in which it has allowed the involvement of special educational need pupils.

From an educational point of view, the main value of the Pushkin Prizes has been the genuine opportunity offered within the mainstream curriculum to pupils to display their talents in creative writing. The Prizes also provide an important cultural opportunity for exchanges between young people from Scotland and St Petersburg.

The Pushkin Prizes scheme has become an established feature of the curriculum in S1 and S2 in Scottish local authority schools and I am sure will continue to be so for years to come.

IAN MILLS

DIRECTOR OF EDUCATION & LEISURE SERVICES

EAST DUMBARTONSHIRE COUNCIL

I write from my head. Images and words collect there like dew on a spring day. When I write, I can imagine the scene, the characters and the action as if it was a film in my mind . . . I almost always imagine what's going to happen next before I write it, the next sentence forming in my head, and I can see it as if it was really happening . . . Story-writing is my life, I write them all the time. It's only the daunting task of converting them onto paper that stops me doing more. The Pushkin Prizes were like a target, I had a reason to put some of the stories in my head onto paper. I enjoyed having the opportunity to write about anything I wanted, as well.

KIRSTI MCGREGOR

QUEENSFERRY HIGH SCHOOL

Out of My Window

Out of my window,
The chimneys all stand,
Like a crowd of fat ladies.
The smoke gushes out:
A cloud of words!

The pylons reach up
So high, they touch clean sky,
They send visions of me
When I stretch or yawn.

Houses are built:
An overlapping patchwork quilt,
That's dusty and fading,
And should be thrown out.

The wires are entangled,
They wind themselves right round:
A spiral staircase
Leading to the sky.

If these things
Were as I imagine them,
I'd put them to use
And climb to Heaven,
Straight from Hell.

MARIE DAVIE
LAWSIDE ACADEMY, DUNDEE
HIGHLY COMMENDED, 1990/91

My Reflection

When I look in the mirror
all I see,
Is another person staring back
at me.
She looks like me,
She talks like me,
But is this image all I see?

Might she be another being,
Fighting to get out,
Wanting to be free?
And what does she do when I'm not there?
Does she sit behind her glass prison
and stare?
Like an ant trapped under a glass,
Does she sit and sob while other people
pass?

Oblivious to all her tears
Does she have ideas, hopes and fears?
Does she dream of love and hate?
Or does she only sit and wait?
"Wait for what?" I hear you cry.
For what will become of her the day I die?
Will she be trapped an old woman or
will she be free
From her glass prison eternally?

EVE KEIGHLEY

PERTH ACADEMY

SECOND PRIZE, 1990/91

One Day My Prince Won't Come

Imagine, seven daughters in seven years! And six of the sisters were so beautiful, tall and slender, with long golden curls. The seventh child was the runt of the family: small, stunted, pale skin and red hair; and as ugly as can be. The six pretty sisters teased the littlest one, so that she stormed and shouted.

Her father stormed and shouted too, telling her she was more trouble than all the others put together. Her father didn't love her. Her mother said she loved her so much why couldn't she be good and sweet like her sisters? Then the seventh child would feel so wretched she would creep out into the garden and cry.

She was weeping there one day when she saw a line of ants scurrying across the sandy path; little black wriggling ants. She stood where she was, wondering if they would scurry across her bare feet. But the ants advanced carefully along the edge of one foot, and came to a halt, making a special shape. There was no mistaking it. It was a seven.

The next day she went into the garden for another weep, and the same thing happened. And the next day and the next and the next two days after that. And on the seventh day they spoke. "Do not weep, seventh sister," they said. "Wait seven more years and then we will see what we will see."

This cheered the seventh sister though she felt she was in for a rather long wait.

That year the eldest sister had her fourteenth birthday. She had grown so lovely, that all the boys in the village clumped round to the cottage to woo her. The eldest sister smiled but shook her golden head. Then one day a handsome prince came galloping by. When he saw the eldest sister he was bewitched by her beauty. He beckoned to her onto the back of his white steed and took her for a little ride. And then another little ride. And another. And another. And then one day they galloped off into the sunset and perhaps they lived happily ever after.

The next year the second eldest sister had her fourteenth birthday. She had grown so lovely that all the village boys clumped round to woo her. But she smiled and shook her long golden head (after dallying with a few in case her prince didn't come). But, one day, along he came and they rode off into the sunset, and perhaps they lived happily ever after too.

And the same thing happened to the next sister and the next; and the next two after that. But the ants kept on making the same shape time and time again, always muttering the same thing. And then the seventh sister was fourteen. But she hadn't grown any lovelier, and the village boys clumped right on past her but she did not lose faith. She just went back to work muttering, "We will see what we will see."

And one day sure enough, a handsome prince came trotting up to the cottage on a milk-white steed. A really highborn prince with all the correct royal regalia (some of the other princes had been a bit suspect, very flash in white satin shirts and red leather buckled boots). The seventh child was in the garden pulling up vegetables for supper. She quickly threw the carrots to the ground and rubbed her earthy hands on her apron. She stared up at the handsome prince and just for a second she really did seem to blossom: eyes shining, hair flowing. But the prince was looking up at the window at her mother who was brushing her long golden hair. And the prince was bewitched by her beauty. He beckoned to her to come down and join him on his horse. And she did, still lovely and lithe even though she had borne seven children. And the way they looked at each other as they rode off into the sunset, it was obvious they were never coming back.

Her father went to the pub to get drunk, but she picked up the carrots and stood on the ants.

LUCY PIPER

THE ROYAL HIGH SCHOOL, EDINBURGH

SECOND PRIZE, 1992/93

The Girl on the Roof

There was a girl who was very beautiful and also very vain.
So she sat on the roof of her house to get attention from the pretty birds.
As they flew by she would smooth her hair and they would all look,
And chirp, "How beautiful you are!"
But none would stop.
Being told she was beautiful should have made the girl happy,
But it didn't.

Instead she began to moan because she couldn't fly freely as the
    little birds did,
And soon the few friends she used to have drifted away in a little boat,
And she didn't notice.
So she never came off the roof,
And she began to lose her beauty because the strong winds blew it away,
And the rain washed it off.
She never sheltered.
And still when the little birds flew by she would smooth her hair,
But they turned their heads away in disgust at her ugliness.
She became unhappy and at last went searching for the ladder
    she had climbed onto the roof with,
But somebody had taken it away because they thought she didn't
    want it anymore.
The girl began to cry because she didn't want to be stuck on the roof,
She kept thinking of her friends cosy and warm together in their little boat,
Sailing away to new times and leaving her in their past.
She longed to be with them because she was so cold and alone,
But everybody thought the moans were just the wind,
And the tears were just the rain,
So nobody came to help her,
Because they couldn't see her, so high up.
And anyway,
They thought she liked it.

SUSAN RADCLIFFE, DUMFRIES HIGH SCHOOL

FIRST PRIZE (EQUAL), 1995/96

False Teeth Overboard

TEETH! Who needs them? We all do, even if they are false ones! Those who are lucky enough to have our real teeth have never experienced what my great-grandfather experienced!

(This story has been passed down by my great-grandfather to my grandfather, to my mother and then (finally) to me. It took place on the island of Lewis, in a place called 'Back'.)

"*Maduinn Mhath!*" called Murdo to his old companion and good friend Calum. Murdo was white-haired and had light blue eyes. His stooped shoulders, once broad and strong, made him look older than he really was and his white beard added to his age, although without it he would have lost some of his character.

Calum was younger than Murdo, but not by much. He was 65 years of age, and preferred not have a beard. . . His main hobby was fishing. He fished every day, if the sun was high, and he swore that the sea always gleamed when it was a day for fish.

"So, Calum, are we going fishing this afternoon?

"Of course! I told you that today would be a good day! Oh Murdo, I forgot to tell you," Calum went on, "Donald is coming with us this afternoon. He just sort of invited himself along."

Murdo groaned. "Oh! Not that old windbag! He's getting too old to come fishing with us 'young people'."

"Now, now, Murdo," retorted Calum, "pull yourself together and give the man some respect. He's only a few years older than us - and he has a lot more brains than you, anyway!"

"Och!" protested Murdo. "He's just such a moan!"

"Sssh!!" whispered Calum. "Here he comes now! I don't want him to hear what you're saying about him. You know he wouldn't like it."

Old Donald shuffled slowly over to them, greeted them in Gaelic and then, with a long groan, sat down on an overturned stone and gazed at them expectantly. Donald had been in the army, and had lost a lot of good friends, relatives and loved ones in his lifetime. Everyone said he didn't smile at all because of these tragedies. But Murdo knew the truth! He KNEW the truth! The truth was that Donald didn't smile because he didn't want to. Unlike Murdo, Donald had absolutely NO sense of humour, and seemed to get out of bed on the wrong side every day. Murdo stared at Donald and wondered if he had ever seen him smile or laugh. Suddenly, Donald sneezed, and blew noisily into a grubby handkerchief.

"My, that's a bad cold you've got there, Donald," said Calum. Donald answered with another sneeze. After some time his hoarse voice reached their ears.

"So, when are we going out then?" he asked slowly. . .

Half-an-hour later Murdo, Donald and Calum were down at the shore, where their boat was tied with a rope on to a strong stake stuck hard and deep into the sand. Donald sat himself down on a large boulder, and left Calum and Murdo to get on with it. . .

"Leaving us to do everything!" muttered Murdo under his breath. "Why should he just sit there and do nothing?". . .

Pretty soon, though, the boat was ready to go. With many a creak and a groan, she set off on the calm, blue waters that stretched as far as the eye could see. They sailed in silence, broken only by the sound of the waves breaking on to the shore, and occasionally the shriek of seagulls overhead.

Murdo stole a glance at Donald and was surprised to see the old man looking around with obvious happiness in his heart, and a smile on his face! Then he caught sight of Murdo watching him, and the smile vanished. Murdo looked quickly away.

PLOP! Murdo's line went into the sea, followed by another 'plop '- then a sneeze from Donald. . . Donald threw his fishing line down into the sea, and then seemed to doze off. Everything was so peaceful and calm. Murdo watched the sunlight sparkling on the deep, blue water. His sigh was one of pure happiness.

Suddenly, the quiet atmosphere was shattered by the most enormous sneeze ever heard in the entire universe! AAAATISHOOO!! And when Donald sneezed, the top set of his false teeth flew out of his mouth, and with a small splash, plunged into the ocean. Donald stared aghast at the small ripples that were spreading across the sea. Murdo tried hard to conceal his laughter, as Donald started desperately fishing around in the water for his teeth. Calum stuffed a hanky into his mouth, to quieten his own laughter, and both of them wondered what would happen next!

Just then, Murdo had a bright idea. He nudged Calum and asked him to occupy Donald for a few moments. Calum was puzzled, but seeing the look on Murdo's face, he obeyed. Murdo turned away from them, and slipped his OWN false teeth out. He put them into a hand-net and gently lowered it over the side.

"Now Donald, cheer up!" Murdo called cheerfully across the boat. "I'll fish around and try to see if I can find your teeth with my net here." Donald stared at the sea hopelessly. Calum gasped as he looked at Murdo's toothless grin and realised what he was up to. "No, no!" Calum seemed to say. Murdo fished around for a while and then brought up the hand-net. As it came up Donald looked at it eagerly, and gave a howl of delight.

"MY TEETH! MY TEETH!" he cried. He grabbed them quickly and stuck them back into his mouth. Murdo was enjoying the joke so much he let it go on - for too long. Donald's delight changed to a look of dismay, because as soon as the teeth were in, they were out again. "Och!!" he shouted angrily, flinging the teeth back out to sea as far as he could. "These ones weren't mine! They must have belonged to some other poor soul!" He sat back crossly in his seat and stared at the other two glumly.

Murdo . . . was too shocked to say anything! Calum, though, couldn't hold in his laughter. He laughed and laughed until the tears ran down his cheeks. After some time Murdo could do no more than join in, and started to laugh as well. Only Donald remained grumpy, and couldn't of course understand why the other two were laughing so much! Between laughter and tears, Calum explained it to him.

Donald looked at Murdo. Murdo grinned at Donald. The corners of Donald's mouth turned up slightly, then all the way up, and then came a laugh, and finally roars of laughter, filling the whole bay. They forgot their fishing and went home. The news spread around the small village like wildfire. How they all laughed at Donald and Murdo, but Donald and Murdo didn't really mind as they had done so much laughing themselves. In fact, they became firm friends after that afternoon, and often reminded each other of that episode out on the bay, all those years ago!

ISABEL STONE

THURSO HIGH SCHOOL

HIGHLY COMMENDED, 1996/97

Childhood

It was wrong! I couldn't help it.
Fed up chewing red paint
Off the playpen!
I scrambled over
And landed with a thud,
Shuffled into her room.

Oh beautiful dressing table!
Oh beautiful, beautiful bag!
Velvet soft with little diamonds.
Wriggling fingers pulled
The purple zip,
 - Shlip!-
An explosion on the floor.

A red crayon
Shiny, smooth smells of Mum.
I rub, rubbed all over my face.
What fun!
Then powdery taste,
Bright blue, on tip of nose
And red, red paint
On fingers and toes.

"Rachel, what are you doing?"
Her screwed up face
made me shudder
As a cloth rubbed off the colour.
All of a sudden I was in the tub
Rub, rub, rub-a-tub-dub!
After, in a big soft towel,
She wrapped me in her love.

RACHEL FREEMAN, THE ROYAL HIGH SCHOOL, EDINBURGH

HIGHLY COMMENDED, 1994/95

Angel in the Library

When the boy came in
all turned and stared.
Mouths opened, teeth flickered
and computers stared.

Back down the corridor
the little boy ran.
Book carrying giants loped past.
Some turned around,
but the little boy
was never found.

An angel tall and strong
winging its way toward
the little boy.
Such a groaning and a moaning.
"Where's my mummy?"
And the angel whispered
his sweet answer.

CHRISTOPHER PEGGIE

Any Old Night of the Week

As the car pulled away from the front of the flats it left the building looming large over everything. A gust of wind swept up and then dropped litter over the paved forecourt.

The building stood as silent as a tree.

Its balconies deserted like a closed theatre.

And then the structure leapt back into life. Cats meowed and dogs barked, splitting the thick grey silence.

A pale-faced boy, not very old, wearing a filthy denim jacket, peered over a balcony.

A group of bigger boys on the ground huddled around a small, defenceless puppy. The puppy howled as the boys took turns to kick it from one to another. Encouraged by its howls of agony, they carried on with their torment.

A glass bottle flashed as it flew down from the second floor balcony and the little boy's hand fluttered out of sight again.

A scream of pain pierced the city air. A large, wellbuilt redhead clutched at his arm before crumpling like a piece of paper.

The puppy, seizing its chance, scampered through the ring of booted feet.

But the gang leader had already scanned the building with his cold blue eyes. His search ended as a tuft of blond hair wavered above the balcony on the second floor left.

As the gang flowed up the stairs, a small shivery dog stayed close to the wall as it made its skitterish way to the forecourt, where it joined its pack-mates foraging in the bins.

The little boy raced past boarded-up flats and along the glass-strewn walkway. His wordless prayer was answered! The lift was working tonight! He almost yelped in relief.

He bolted out into the night and charged straight into a uniformed constable. The policeman pushed the boy out to arm's length and looked down at him.

"I want to go home!" wept the boy.

CHRISTOPHER PEGGIE

Alone

Again
They were there,
The four black knights,
And he was alone.

The knights shimmered
Four scarlet dragons
at their back.
And he was alone.

A muddied blazer.
Four red tears
Tore his face,
And he was alone.

For them
No blame, no shame,
Nothing.
And he was alone.

Please Mum,
Don't phone,
The knights stood bowed,
But only for a moment,
And he was alone.

CHRISTOPHER PEGGIE

THE ROYAL HIGH SCHOOL, EDINBURGH

SECOND PRIZE, 1993/94

Trapped

Peter looked out into space, through the bars that made one wall of the cell, grabbing the cold iron as if willing it to melt in his hands. . . The cold, hard walls surrounded him, mocked him. He fell back with a groan.

There was a heavy, ominous silence, as if the whole universe was waiting for something to happen. His eyes travelled across to the huge American in the corner. He looked at him with a deep hatred, as if it was he who had framed him. . . The woman sat a few feet away. Behind the tousled red hair, the blood and dirt-stained face and clothes had a picture of calmness. He glanced towards the other corner at a heap of misery. Thin as a rake, tiny and mucky, the wretch lay. His thick, oily black hair was crawling with lice and the rags that he wore were hanging on like a thread. Worst of all was the face, the lifeless, glaring mask with pitch-black eyes. Eyes that reflected no light. Eyes that were staring at him.

. . . Peter lay awake going over the past day in his mind. The arrest, the imprisonment, the silence, the eyes. He shuddered and tried to shake off the image.

He drifted into a troubled sleep. He was in a maze and Death was after him. Every time he turned a corner it was there, with those eyes. For hours he ran, before collapsing in a heap. He lay there and looked up at Death. With the American's face. The scythe descended. . .

Peter was wakened the next morning by the clatter of the door opening. In marched half a dozen guards. Hauling him to his feet, they marched him out of the cell and down the main corridor. Towards the door. Hope surged through him as he saw the American and the woman were outside. Free! A huge grin spread across his face as they approached the open door but the guards just laughed and dragged him down another passageway. That wouldn't stop him. This was his chance to be free. Elbowing a guard in the face, he sped away and leapt out of the door, whooping with joy. Before he was halfway along the street he heard the red-haired woman shouting "Don't!" and felt a flash of searing pain as the bullets dug into his back. He fell to the ground. He looked up and there was the American looking down at him.

JAMIE RODGER, CRIEFF HIGH SCHOOL

FIRST PRIZE, 1989/90

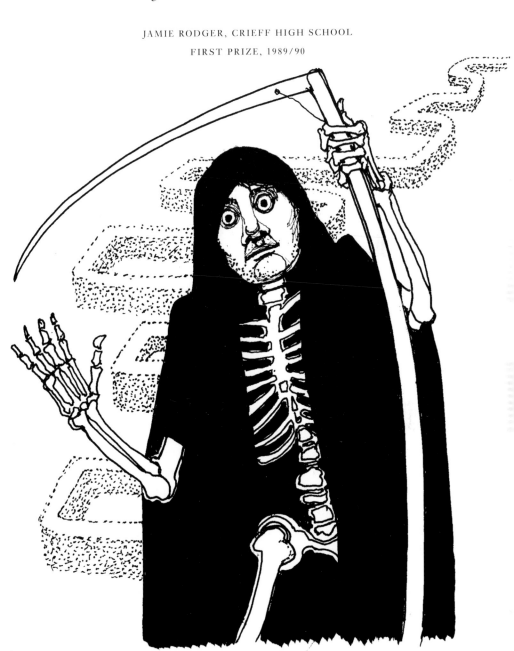

Mama

Sitting in the cramped, bleak room was like sitting in a cold version of hell . . . My bald head ached as the wind breezed past it, through the tiny square hole at the top of the wall. My brown, dusty skin was wrinkled even though I was only fourteen. It was wrapped tight around my cheekbones and my lips were dry and cracked. The blue overall-type suit I wore was hanging on me as I was so thin. The yellow star on my sleeve smelled of mould and was peeling off at the top . . .

Suddenly, we heard the distinctive sound of padlocks 'clunking' and doors slamming. Immediately we all sat up, wide-eyed . . . The door of the room was flung open and the Nazi soldier's mean staring eyes scowled at us. His voice echoed off the walls, deafening me.

He spoke directly to me. "You will be taken outside! Outside with all your - friends." His eyes were like slits. In return I glared back at him, meeting stare for stare.

"Get up!"

I hesitated. He gripped me by the shoulders and heaved me up. The rough contact brought an image, a flashback of my parents being dragged away through the streets of Uzhgorod, further and further away from me. The vivid memory was too much for me. I lashed forward, attempting to hit out at the Nazi. Futile. He simply put his hand out and cupped it around my head while I struggled, clawing in mid-air. He flung me away. I backed off, mortified.

The soldier now marched us through the damp, dark corridors of the camp. The walls were chipped and cracked. As we walked out to the dusty grounds, a woman caught the corner of my eye. She was gripping on to the cage-like fence that surrounded us. Her face was strained, grimacing. A conspicuous Christian silver cross hung around her neck. She was shouting and crying, pointing at us.

Our heads were turned round brusquely by the guard. We were not to see what was going on . . . But the shouting of the woman seemed to drown out everything.

"That's my child!" she screamed. "I swear on the Holy Bible! Please believe me! She should not be in here. She was brought up a Christian and always will be a Christian!"

I glanced right and left. Who was she pointing at? Not me??
She was screaming at one of the guards. He began shouting at our guard in the brash German they always spoke.

"*Diese Frau, sie sagt, das Mädchen ist* **ihres** *Kind!*" Before I knew it, I was whisked off, dragged like a rag doll by my shoulder.

I was standing in a room in front of the Commandant, sinister, sitting up very straight behind a huge, mahogany desk. I could see my scared face in its marble sheen. Two soldiers stood erect by the door. The atmosphere in that room was colder than the chill outside.

The door was pulled open by the soldiers and the woman from the fence walked in, gripped roughly by a guard. She looked petrified. . . Our eyes met. Hers were a wispy, dull grey and they seemed to be telling me something; willing me to understand.

She shook herself free from the guard and came running towards me as if to fling herself on me, but was restrained by the soldiers. Then she began screaming and wailing in frustrated despair:

"Sie ist mein Kind. Sie ist ein christliches Kind. Ihre Soldaten haben sie weggenommen, als sie mit einigen jüdischen Kinder gespielt hat. Geben sie mir meine Tochter zurück!!"

Her child? I wasn't her child. The woman was mad! I didn't know what she was babbling about. I took a closer look at her face. No, I had never seen her in my life, I was sure! She looked me straight in the eyes again – and then I understood.

The realisation that this woman was ready to risk her life to save me was overwhelming . . . Struggling desperately to sound convincing, I said, "Mama?" I received a reassuring smile. She gave a sigh of relief.

"Gretchen . . . ," she said. I was so nervous . . . In all this danger I found myself thinking how strange it was, liking being in the presence of a Christian. Mother had always told me not to speak to Christians.

The soldiers made it worse, staring at me, interrogating us, threatening us . . . They were getting nowhere. She calmly stuck to her story. I had been playing with some Jewish children when the soldiers arrived.

Finally the Commandant sat back in his chair, defeated. His arms were folded right up against his chest, now more like a child with a temper. . . Just when I though he had given up, he suddenly leapt forward and thudded his fists on the desk.

"And what exactly do you think you are going to do with your so-called 'Gretchen', eh?"

"Why, take her home to her brothers and sister of course," she replied confidently.

He had lost and he knew it. He flopped back in his chair again, staring at my 'identity papers' on his blotter.

"Take her," he said to the desk.

"But. . . !"

"TAKE HER! Take her away from me. NOW!"

It was incredible! Was I really going home with this woman? Would she really be my Mama?

She put her welcoming arms around me and we walked slowly out of that cold, desolate place which had been my only home for so long . . .

So you see, Chana, you are my namesake. When my saviour called me 'Gretchen', I had to keep that name for safety. The name 'Chana' disappeared until my son gave me a granddaughter.

But Gran. . .

Yes?

Don't you miss your real Mother – and your Father?

Oh I do miss them, I miss them dearly, but they have found peace. I will remember and love them always.

What happened to the other children, Gran?

I don't know, my Chana. I tried to find out after the war, but it was impossible. I don't know why Mama saved me out of all those wretched souls.

Perhaps God chose for us to be together.

DANA SWANSON

QUEENSFERRY HIGH SCHOOL

HIGHLY COMMENDED, 1995/96

Rapids

The dashing white sergeants
In their glistening white uniforms
On parade in the morning sunlight,
using the river beds for roads
Moving their troops along.
The troops, tired by their descent
From the snow-capped hills,
Rapidly flood into the enemy.
Silently they disappear
Never to be heard from again.
But still they come,
Brave, courageous and strong
Still losing the battle
Though their source of troops is never ending.
Still they come
To give support to their comrades
But yet, their whole army cannot withstand
The power of the sea, their enemy.
They attack in vain
Again, again; but still
They drown.

KEVIN WILLIAMSON, ARBROATH HIGH SCHOOL
SECOND PRIZE, 1991/92

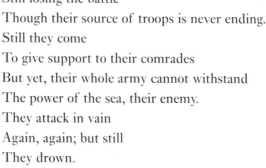

Mr Clayton

Somewhere in Derbyshire a primary class are having the time of their lives. I know this because their teacher is a Mr Clayton. He is an inspired teacher, one of the few who really make a difference. He came to our small school in Bearsden for two years and changed the lives of the pupils who were lucky enough to be in his class. He knew that learning should be fun, and for them it certainly was. For the year that our class had him, he shared his life with us, and we shared ours with him.

I can still remember him coming in, dressed conventionally in a green jacket and black trousers. However, a Sylvester the Cat tie was just visible under the jacket. In retrospect we should have seen this as a huge wink, a hint of fun to come, an indication of his perverse sense of humour. . .

He sat down at the desk and decided to start with the ground rules. "Right, then, class 6A, we are stuck with each other for the rest of the year. I intend to enjoy myself and I hope you will, too. This year will be fun if you follow three simple rules: do your work, always listen to me, and don't make fun of my name, because I was born with it." This was different from previous teachers, who all held the view of a former era, that 'children should be seen and not heard'.

He stayed in a small flat in the West End of Glasgow, which by his own account was a dump. This flat was apparently the scene of many escapades. One night he was locked out, so he had to come to school dressed in friends' clothes. On another occasion, when he had overslept, he came to school still wearing his pyjama top under his jumper. He said there was no need for a kitchen, as he knew the numbers of the home delivery Chinese, Pizza and Indian restaurants. One day he had to walk to school in torrential rain. He stood up on a chair, asked for our attention and proceeded to flex his old leather trainers, resulting in a pool of the most putrid water you have ever seen flowing on to the floor.

An ardent football fan, he would often stop the maths lesson and start talking about the struggle of his home team, Derby. He would always make us laugh and maybe we would spend half the lesson talking to him; but for the rest of the time we did four times as much work as we normally would. As he got to know us better he became a bit more familiar. For example, he would have his breakfast every morning – a roll with a packet of salt and vinegar crisps in it. I still have a vivid recollection of the day when two raucous seagulls decided to peck vociferously on our annexe roof. This was destroying the attention of the class. After some time of trying to endure the tapping, Mr Clayton finally gave up. He leapt out onto the balcony brandishing a broom and screeching like a demented monkey, trying to scare them off.

On another day we were having a class debate on the punishment of someone who will remain nameless for legal reasons. Mr Clayton decided to give the accused a proper hearing. To play the part of the judge he put the blackboard duster on his head. I got the part of lawyer for the defence. At this point the janitor walked by the window. Casually Mr Clayton smiled and gave him a regal wave, as if it was entirely normal for a teacher to wear a duster on his head.

That year was not all in a happy tone for me. There were three boys in the class who didn't like me. I was quite new to the school and an easy target.

I don't want to go to school today. Familiar sounds seem strangely distant, I am carrying a lead weight around. I play with my breakfast, uninterested. My Mum keeps asking if there is something wrong. I can't answer because I don't know myself, can't quite put it into words. They will be there again behind me in class. They push my books off my desk every time Mr Clayton's back is turned. They call me names even though I have asked them to stop. I am in a dilemma. Do I tell and chance it getting worse, or do I just let it go on and see if it goes away? I can't stand this constant baiting any longer. I decide that I am going to tell, but will he believe me? Will he be able to stop it or to do anything? I told him, and for once I saw a streak of anger in his eyes. I really don't know what he did but it worked.

I recently ventured into the cupboard with all the school photographs and found the picture from that year. He had an innocent grin like an angel, with no indication of his actual personality; but for us who knew him, there is a glint in his eye that we can all remember.

In that year I acquired a number of essential tools for life. I learned about Pythagoras' theorem and the line-up of the Derby football team. I perfected the art of watercolour painting and I now have a bowling arm action to rival any county side player. I realised that learning can be fun and people can only help if they know how you are feeling! Mr Clayton had stayed in Scotland because he was going to get married to a Scottish girl. For some reason they split up and so he left. That brings us back to the class in Derbyshire. They are out there somewhere and I would desperately like to know something: does he still have that tie?

EWAN LOWE

BOCLAIR ACADEMY, BEARSDEN

FIRST PRIZE, 1996/97

To Harry

When I walked through the cold school
In the morning
No one there but me
and the buzzing of the lights in the Dinner Hall
I would listen
To the footsteps
of a warm hearted man
I would turn and say
"Hello"
He would surely stay
And have a talk
Anytime.

Yes
It's hard to think
that when I walk
In the cold school
I know he's
Harry's
Not there
But a warm breeze is there
Forever
People come
people go
Why Harry?
I'll never know
Sometimes
It's just hard
to let go.

LAWRENCE EATON

INVERALMOND COMMUNITY HIGH SCHOOL

SPECIAL ENDEAVOUR AWARD 1997

Ees Too Cold!

Deer Seer,

I José el Parrot, am writink to complain about thees terreeble country. Eet ees wet, cold and most of all ees too cold!

I was mindink mine own business, flying around mine home the jungle. Then, I is seeing one beautiful parrot. I theenks I weel check her out no? So, I ees going over expecting a beeg kees and what am I getting? A beeg hand reachink for mine weengs and cleeping those off! I cannot be flyink off now I theenks, and I iss right! Then I iss being sacked as you say, no? Ah bagged that ees the word, I iss bagged and I iss finding myself een a beeg crate. Eet was none of the good I can tell you! Eet was cramped and smellee. I am running into parrots whom I have not seen for years and I am being told we are being sheeped to Breetain. There, we weel be put into leetle cages and saying, "Polly wants a cracker" and "Preety Boy" and the like. I am asking you would you seet around awl day talking of peegsbubble like that! So, I is taken to the Pet Shop where they expect you to be saying, "Geev us a kees" and other ver seely theengs. Eet ees diabolical!!!! They geeve us theengs like sunflower seeds and the like. Not a beet of decent food!

So een one day ees coming a leetle boy. I is theenking he ees not looking so bad as the other yukkee people who have been comink een (Eef I do not like them I ees using my beak so they has very sore feengers by the time I ees feenished weeth them) I ees liking the look of thees leetle boy so I am keepeeng mine beak to mine own self. Hees mumee ees forking out her own cash for me!

Anyway he ees very good to me. He ees teaching me theengs like times tables, heestory dates and funee rhymes. But then he ees not there! They all pack up and leave me! I open mine leetle cage and I ees off! You are not seeing me round there no more. But I soon deescover thees ees not a very good country. Ees wet and there ees none of the fresh air I am liking so much But most of all EES TOO COLD!

Yours unhappeely

José el Parrot

P.S I ees on my way back to mine beautiful home now. There ees no need for any of thees worryeeng to be done about me.

AMY GUNNING
ST JOHN'S HIGH SCHOOL, DUNDEE
COMMENDED 1993/94

My World of Pushkin

I live in St Petersburg, on Pushkin Street, and when I was a little child, Father walked with me in a small public garden, where the poet's monument stands. I ran around it, and tried to climb up the pedestal. So I got acquainted with Pushkin.

Father often told me about him. I learned that Pushkin wrote poems, loved the people very much and defended the weak people in his poems. And then he was killed. And after that they remembered how good he was and decided to erect the monument.

At home Mom read Pushkin's fairy tales to me. Then I heard wonderful stories about the toys, which we hung on the fir-tree before the New Year: about the Golden Cock and Shamahan Princess, Small Izba on Hen's Legs and Tsar Saltan. . .

When I began to read myself, I discovered Pushkin's poems about nature. I imagined brooks, forests and fields, described by the poet. When I read *Storm* I thought of an old small hut with a ramshackle roof; around it, a snow storm is raging and an old nurse is sitting inside and spinning; behind her the young poet is sitting at the table and writing with the help of a lamp's light. It is dry and warm in the hut. . .

Now I often walk along Nevsky Prospect. I imagine how it must have looked more than one and a half centuries ago. In the evening carriages rushed along the Prospect, the cabmen shouted, making noise and mess. One carriage had stopped just near the sidewalk. A foppishly dressed young man with a top hat came out of it. That was Onegin, hurrying to the ball at the Anichkov palace.

I also go often to the Anichkov palace. In the halls, where discos and concerts take place now, there were magnificent court balls, which Kammerjunker Pushkin and his wife attended. Probably, he stood at a corner, leaned on a column. Often the poet was bored, but sometimes his face lit up and again he was willing to admire Beauty and to create. And today, nearly two hundred years afterwards, Pushkin stirs my imagination.

Pushkin has given me a great wonderful world, into which I can always look.

SERGEY HELMAN

SCHOOL NO.209, ST PETERSBURG. COMMENDED, 1993/94

The Dogs Keep Silence
out of Being Tactful

Every evening I walk with my dog, the black kolly. I walk for a long time and go slowly in the dark park. In those minutes I'm not lonely. I begin to talk with my dog and the dog answers me. . .

– Set me free. Why are you holding me? Kolly asked.

– I'm afraid you'll run away. There are other dogs.

– Don't worry. I'll not run.

– Why do people lead dogs on something long? – he asked.

– Because a man doesn't trust his dog. He is afraid that his dog will leave him.

– What does 'will leave' mean? – wondered Kolly.

– To leave means that somebody leaves someone alone, it's when you'll never see the one who left you, and you'll never hear his voice, and you can't jump on him with your front paws and lick him.

– I'll never leave you – he said – And what about you?

– You are my dog and I love you.

– Don't know what that is, 'I love'.

– 'I love' is what you feel when you have a dream about the dog, when you have a dream how you play with it or when you do it when awake. It is when you feel straining emotions. When you love, you can overcome any barrier. . . There is no happiness without love. For me, my happiness is you, because I love you. But love can be different. My parents love each other and it is another kind of love.

– Tell me about your parents. I don't remember my parents.

– Parents are people to whom you often go for caress, they love both you and me. Parents are my masters. They are people who feed me, who talk to me, they are people with whom I'm happy. My mother caresses me, and I feel similar pleasure which you feel when somebody strokes you. When I remember about my parents I go home faster.

– Go home? I often hear this. What is the word?

– Home is where you are free. It may seem nomad dogs have an absolute freedom, but this freedom is already loneliness. . . Home protects me as well as you, my dog, protect our home. Home is the place where a person returns and turns into a real 'himself'. Home is the place where dogs and people take off a collar. I would embrace my home if I could do that, as little children embrace their soft toys. . .

It was so quiet around. Leaves fell down and it was possible to hear their rustling. When Kolly kept silence it seemed to me that I was talking with myself.

– Every day – he continued – when I'm at home alone I think why people take dogs but I can't answer this question.

– The dearest on the earth is the feeling of responsibility for someone. You are my friend and I'm responsible for you before our bonds. I'm responsible for your happiness.

– I am responsible for you too – Kolly said – When I play with you and bite your hand with love I'm afraid to make you pain. I'm a free dog, because I belong to you.

– You feel yourself free because you aren't alone. Loneliness is a cage.

[35]

Life loses its sense when a man is in solitude, because he doesn't have to speak sincerely with somebody and has nobody to open his heart to. He'll never feel relief because he has nobody to share his ache. . .

So it was quite dark. I looked at the watch.

- It is time to return. It's late.

We stopped.

- Why do you depend on time - asked Kolly - why do you look at the watch before going back home?

- Your life is time too - I said - which you must use at your discretion. People like accuracy, so they invent a watch. Every day you wait for me at a particular time and if I'm late you begin to worry.

- But I have a feeling when you should come, without knowing time. And now you looked at the watch because you feel unwell, you are bored, you are tired? Is it so? For when a man is fine and he is happy he forgets about the time.

I felt my hands grow cold. I answered with passion:

- I've done this because I know they are waiting for me. When somebody is waiting for you, you must go.

- If I had a watch I would break it - he said - It is rather cold. But we must go, I feel it now.

- Let's go - I said.

- Let's go - answered Kolly.

We went and the trees that had heard all that stayed behind.

MIKHAIL PESOCK, SCHOOL NO.105, ST PETERSBURG

HIGHLY COMMENDED, 1992/93

[36]

The Circles (extract)

It was about ten years back from now in Elgin - twelfth of June to be precise, when the crop circles started appearing up at the farm. In fact I can still remember the news that night about it all. There were a number of possible explanations, some likelier than others, but no one knew the truth. Still no one knows the truth, but this story is about a group of villagers (myself included) determined to find the truth, and the things that happened to them as they searched for the cause of 'the circles'.

It was a couple of weeks since the first sightings at Rayhead farm and was getting on for half-eleven when the farmer's boy Craig burst into the Black Lion where we were all gathered.

"Come! Come!" he cried, out of breath, "for I fear the worst. Up at the farm there's been a disturbance. Angus is missin' an' we need a search party for there ain't enough folk up there." Davey was the first up, followed by the rest of the lads. Pete and I stayed behind to help clear up the spilled drink and dropped cigars.

"I suppose we'd better tell the wives that their husbands'll be late back," said Pete with a sigh. "Aye," said I. "Or they'll be up all night worryin', the poor souls."

We trudged out leaving Jock the barman to finish the chores, and just glimpsed a bunch of men in Geordie caps, torches in hand, hurrying up the hill as fast as their old legs would carry them. After calling at several houses I said goodnight to Pete and started to walk home. . .

I had not gone twenty yards when I stopped and turned round. Curiosity was heavily plaguing me and I decided to head for the farm and discover what was going on. I set off at half-run, got there in ten minutes, and immediately spotted the group of torches not far off in the middle of the fields. I headed for them and eased my way to the front. There before my eyes lay Angus Macleod, lying in a ready-made grave, in the middle of a circle made from flattened crops.

"From now on," announced Old Davey, "none of us is ower safe."

ANDREW HAWKE, BALERNO COMMUNITY HIGH SCHOOL
FIRST PRIZE (EQUAL), 1994/95

The Auld Ploo Horse

The shire mare stan's in hir harness wi' brasses,
Fresh mornin' dew seeps to the grund fae the grasses,
'Tween traces she hauls the ploo wi' great pow'r,
Fae mornin' throu noon tae the lousin' ho'er.

The muckle mare's sides are a' sweaty an' heavin',
Fae acres o' furras ahent hir she's leavin',
Hir feathers o' silk a' matted wi' gutters,
"Weel lass yir a sicht," the auld fairmer mutters.

The end o' a harsh lang day his come,
The collar an' breechin an' traces undun,
A kind pat on hir quarters, "Git up las yer hame,
Thirs hay in yer hake, an' a feed pail tae tame."

She lays doon amung the thick barley stra',
Hir sair muscles restin', my it's sae bra',
She snoozes an' dreams o' green pastures an' sun,
Tae the place she'll retire fan hir work is a' dun.

SHARON MACRAE, ARBROATH HIGH SCHOOL
COMMENDED, AND SPECIAL PRIZE FOR ENTRY
IN THE SCOTS LANGUAGE, 1996/97

The Grove

A warm July morning. The sun shone brightly, the crystal water of the lake reflected the fleecy clouds, making arabesques on its smooth surface. The lake was calm. Neither a wind gust, nor a water splash, nor the scream of a disturbed bird broke the harmony of this placid morning. It seemed to me at the moment I could stay on the shore of that lake for the rest of my life.

In the grass just near my foot a grasshopper started its chirring. I was about to pick it up to examine it but the grasshopper jumped away and disappeared. I lay down on my back and began to watch the tops of the pines, their trunks huge and absolutely straight, like ship masts. It was very quiet. Suddenly the silence was broken by a light rustle. A gust of wind reminded me that I was in a northern countryside. But the wind dropped as quickly as it had come.

I bent down, picked up a berry, put it in my mouth. Its slightly sharp and sourish taste refreshed me. Leaning against the warm trunk of a huge pine which smelled of resin, I looked at the water. The ripple on the surface of the lake calmed down and I saw a large, black sheat-fish. It was swimming near the very bottom, slowly moving its long moustaches. A woodpecker settled nearby and started its rhythmic tapping. . .

He hears crashes and discovers that the trees, planted in Peter the First's reign, are being felled, to make way for an electrical power line.

Those ruined trees reminded me of lifeless human bodies and the yellow drops of resin seemed tears to me.

. . . Dozens of trees, hundreds . . . And it seemed to me that all of them were whispering, crying to me, saying that I had to do something. But what should I do? . . . Now I pictured all lumber-men, not in their orange vests, but in executioners' red cloaks.

Last summer together with other schoolchildren I went on an ecological expedition to the old Vespssky Forest. One night, sitting round the crackling camp-fire, we were told a story about ancient Slavs and their attitude to trees. Our ancestors believed that the souls of their dead fellow-tribesmen moved into trees. Therefore it was a great sin to fell an old, tall tree as the soul of some righteous old man dwelled in it.

They never cut down young trees, as they believed that children's souls inhabited them. It was also sinful to cut crooked, weak and squeaky trees, where the souls of sick, unhappy and suffering persons lived. And every time those ancient people had to fell a tree they talked to it, explaining their need for that tree and asking it to forgive them. . .

I took an early suburban train to the city. Yet I wasn't the first to come to the Nature Protection Committee asking for help to protect that grove. It turned out there were some other concerned people who had come there before me and had sounded an alarm. Eventually it was prohibited to fell trees in the groves.

The next year I went to that place again. I met no lumber-men, I didn't see any fallen trees there. There were only the stumps, which had grown dark, and some dry branches with brown needles lying here and there. . . There was no harmony in the forest anymore: the cold wind was raging, the sky was covered with a grey mist and even the water seemed dark and dirty. It was as if the sun had been switched off forever. . .

The rain became stronger, the sky flashed with blinding threads of lightning. The thunder roared with an echo, rumbling. The buzzing of chainsaws, the snapping of fallen trees, their booming contact with the ground, the shouts of the lumber-men, the pain in my knees, the whipping branches. . . Who am I? What am I here for? What's my destiny? At last one thing became clear to me: I am a man living on our Earth together with a lot of other creatures and I must not and never will hurt Nature.

Another year passed. Another warm July morning. . . I was approaching the grove by the familiar path. Nothing disturbed the peace, but I felt something had changed in that forest. Grasshoppers didn't chirr, woodpeckers didn't rattle, when I came to the water's edge I saw no lazy sheat-fish. I walked along the edge of the lake slowly, the sand was mixed with mud and had a dull grey colour. The sky clouded over. I stopped and listened. Something was missing. I listened and listened. And then I realised what was wrong: the trees were silent.

DMITRY KHARLAMPIEV

SCHOOL NO.587

ST.PETERSBURG

SECOND PRIZE, 1996/97

Life in a Prison Cell

It's daurk, awfy daurk in here. Ah cannae see a thing. Wait, wha's there? Ah can hear ye. Ah ken you're there. Ma hert's gowpin, it's loupin oot ma chist. Ah can almaist touch it. But ma boady's numb, far too numb.

It's cauld, freezin cauld. Ma airms are shakkin an ma shanks are aboot fallin aff. Ma een are waterin it's sae cauld, an the air's stinkin. It's mingin in here. It reeks o death an evil. Ah can smell evil a mile awa. The rats dinnae help much though. Ah hate rats. They scurry aboot, gnawing ma banes an chewin ma skin. Ah'm feert, sae feert, ah'm shakkin again.

Ah keep seein shaddas, evil shaddas. Ah can sense it. Soon they'll come and git me. They'll tak me awa an. . . ah dinnae ken whit they'll dae tae me. Ah cannae stoap greetin. Ah keep thinkin, if ah'd just kept ma gub shut. Instead, ah went roon tellin obdae whit tae dae an whaur tae go. It's aw ma ain fault. But ah didnae mean it.

Ah'm wabbit, but ah cannae git tae sleep for aw the noises aroon me. The scurryin of rats, the drippin o blood, the crackin o banes. Ah'm feert. An ah'm fashin aboot ma weans, are they aw richt? God help me, why did ah dae it? Ah'm sae bealin but yit feart o the shaddas, keep seein shaddas. Please, please somebody help me. Git me oot o here. Ah'm crackin up, ah'm share o it. They're soon coming for me. Ah cannae tak it for much langer. Ah huv tae git oot o here!

LEANNE BROWN, BIGGAR HIGH SCHOOL

THIRD PRIZE, 1997/98

Everybody Makes Mistakes

Istared down into the infinite, empty blackness. I was depressed. My life's work had gone. Irritably I moved a tentacle, and instantly the dark void around me was lit up with millions of bright, twinkling stars shining like diamonds. They seemed to be laughing at me.

"Stop it!" I yelled, and immediately, they were all gone and I was left alone. Alone, in a vast and desolate universe of my own creation. I became even more depressed.

Why had my pride and joy, my masterpiece, The Earth, ended? It had taken seven whole days to get it right, the longest I've ever spent on a single work. I conjured up a chair to sit down on and carefully curled my lengthy tail up so that I was comfortable. Becoming more optimistic I took hold of the glass of lemonade that had miraculously appeared beside me, and settled down to think it all out.

There had been water for them to drink. The sun to keep them warm. I had even worked it out so that they all supported each other - some had eaten plants and the others had eaten each other. The plants gave out oxygen and took in carbon dioxide, and most of the others took in oxygen and gave out carbon dioxide. I had worked everything out to the last detail. So what had gone wrong?

I found myself thinking back with pleasure. I recalled the centuries when I watched my creations evolve, equipping themselves with the right weapons to protect themselves from the dangers I had made. Yes, I had admired the polar bears' ingenuity. That white fur had been a really original idea at the time! A shame everybody else had to copy it. I laughed, remembering the occasional spanners I had thrown in the works – the volcanoes, earthquakes and hurricanes – just to see how they would cope. I gave a heavy sigh and sank deeper into the luxurious cushions of my chair. Those were the days!

Suddenly I had it! I sat bolt upright, nearly spilling my drink. . . It seemed so long ago, what had they called themselves? "HUMANS!" I cried out. My voice sounded loud and hollow as it echoed back to me, the only noise in an endless cosmos of silence.

How stupid of me! How could I, the most intelligent life form, creator of everything, have forgotten? Now that I had remembered, it seemed just like yesterday that I created them. At first their pomposity had amused me, it had seemed harmless enough. But then, as they began to expand, to want to know everything and be better than all my other creations, I had become bored with them. The way they had thought themselves to be almost as good as me had irritated me. Some of them had even imagined me to have a body just like theirs!

I grunted with indignation and surrounded myself with tall clear mirrors. After admiring my plump, emerald-green body, flexing the muscles in my long athletic legs and swishing my tail regally, I became even more puzzled as to how those humans could possibly think that I would choose to look like them. Their limp bodies and scrawny necks disgusted me. I shuddered with the memory of them, and it took several more moments of gazing at my own perfect reflection before I recovered from the shock of the memory.

I had left them to their own devices. They had hunted every other animal on The Earth to extinction. They had systematically destroyed all the plant life there was. They had become selfish and thoughtless, upsetting the delicate balance of nature by thinking of nothing but their own needs. They had demolished the ozone layer and used up their resources as if they were the only species on Earth. And now look what had happened – there was no Earth left.

I got up from my chair. There was no point in being down-hearted. It had been a pity, I supposed, – all my other creations had been fine. But everybody makes mistakes, mine being to put humans on The Earth.

With a sudden surge of optimism I realised that I had 'all the time in the world', all the time in eternity in fact! Anyway, what are mistakes for if not to learn from?

I cleared my throat and rolled up my sleeves. "Let there be light!" I boomed, and there was light . . .

THE END
(or should I call it THE BEGINNING?)

REBECCA RYAN, WEBSTER'S HIGH SCHOOL, KIRRIEMUIR

THIRD PRIZE, 1992/93

Gordon is a Lot of People

The room was filled with people with the same earth-coloured hair and stone-coloured grey eyes. They were all wearing the same chestnut glasses. Somebody mounted the platform and shouted, "Stand up the real Gordon," - they could all stand up as each and every one of them is real.

Glasgow housing schemes were home to Gordon for the first few years of his life. He and his friend Kenny McNeil, who was destined for professional football stardom, played football all day long. Together they conjured up many pranks, some at school but the majority played on Gordon's poor, unsuspecting mother.

His mother bought some rather expensive biscuits which was very unusual. As soon as Gordon saw them he recognised his favourite variety. "Oh, no! You didn't buy that kind did you?" he exclaimed with his eyes open as wide as they would go.

"Whatever is wrong with them?" his mother asked, her face aghast as she thought of all the money she had just spent.

"Well, nothing really. I was hearing about them the other day in school, they go rotten within twenty-four hours of opening."

"Are you sure?" his mother said. "I don't remember hearing anything about this."

"I'm sure," he said as he put on his sweet little 'I'm-telling-you-the-truth' face. His mother considered what he had said for a moment and then let him eat the whole packet!

After turning many hairs grey on the heads of his primary teachers he moved on to tackle the huge, rough secondary school and after a year or two there many of his teachers had no hair left because he could be talking and throwing things around the room one minute and getting 100% in an exam the next. In fact he had so many good results that universities had a great deal of difficulty trying to keep him out.

Once he had flown through his degree at university and collected the highest honours possible he completed his teacher training and got his first post not long after he married. Everything was going fine until one day the strangest thing happened . . . Gordon was doing an experiment with aluminium powder, sodium powder and magnesium powder, all mixed together and shaped like a small volcano. The volcano was then heated from underneath. It was meant to explode, but it wasn't meant to be compared with Mount Vesuvius.

Pieces of red hot lava flew up into the air some of which set the ceiling on fire! Although the experiment was in popular demand, even Gordon didn't have the nerve to try it again.

When teaching, Gordon is ultra-strict. It's not a good idea to get on the wrong side of him for very few people who have, have lived to tell the tale. When Gordon is with his family, he is not the same person. He laughs, jokes and in general is very good natured.

Gordon has also climbed many mountains and gone on more than his share of holidays abroad. One year he was extra adventurous. He took his family on an expedition across Europe, visiting many weird and wonderful sights. They started out by car and drove from Calais in the north of France all the way to Barcelona in the north of Spain. They visited anywhere and everywhere from beautiful chateaux to wild and wacky aqua fun parks. . .

Apart from conquering lands, setting ceilings alight and eating biscuits, the next Gordon enjoys good food and fine wines, many of them foreign. Watch him devour anything you care to mention from Scotch pies to caviar. As his stomach walls are made of iron, it's surprising to hear that the only thing he can't stomach is bananas. He tries to cook things but they should never be touched unless the person eating it wants to be in hospital for a month with food poisoning!

The last part of Gordon is reasonably sane, can give advice whenever asked and is good at any school subject, which can sometimes be an advantage. The only slight problem is that if anyone ever asks a question which remotely concerns science, he immediately plunges into an hour long lecture which might concern the question asked and even the answer, but only if you ask him on a good day.

As you can see, Gordon is a lot of people, but who can guess how many people Gordon really is?

SARAH ENGLISH

CLEVEDEN SECONDARY SCHOOL

GLASGOW

COMMENDED, 1993/94

Coincidence

A man with a beard and
a beer can approaches me.
He sits down, his Irish
intonation laughing, offering
me a drink. I don't feel
threatened.
I am reading:
Bette Davis - *Mother Goddam.*

He takes an interest, talks,
asks about her films.
The pigeons flock around
us, uncaring about life and
literature, pecking and
clucking, stabbing viciously.
I am curiously drawn to
this stranger.
He becomes part of my
life for the fifteen minutes
we are together.
I leave.
I will never see him again.
Sometimes I remember and
wonder about him.
Does he think of me?
Probably not. Two different
worlds – different paths.
And the pigeons still
are hungry.

DENISE HERD
GROVE ACADEMY
DUNDEE
HIGHLY COMMENDED, 1989/90

Journey to a New Life

I can remember it like yesterday. If I had the chance now I would go back to Scotland, to Skye where I belong. Canada is majestic and full of excitement and promise, but Skye is my home, and the most unbearable and unbelievable thought is that I will never be able to go back . . .

I woke up with the familiar smell of the fire burning and the fumes wafting up my nose. My mother was always up before me, cooking a hearty breakfast of porridge, oatcakes and bannocks. I just lay there on my bed of heather, which I could feel scratching against my back as I turned, thinking to myself how my life in Skye was so perfect . . . I had all I wanted and needed.

I rose from my bed. The floor was cold, with loose earth scattered from people walking on it. I walked slowly out through the large stone doorway on to the grass in front of our croft.

"Ah, Flora, there ye are. Here was me thinking ye would never rise," said my mother warmly, as she sat stirring the porridge in the large iron pot. I noticed something on the wall, it was a letter. I couldn't read very well, father had tried to teach us but we had never gone to school, so I took it to my mother. It looked very important . . . My mother slowly examined it. "John," she said, calling my father, "come and read this."

My father had been chopping fire wood on a tree stump. He walked over, plucked the piece of paper from my mother's hand and began to read.

To the tenants of the croft Macduigh, on the south side of Skye, Mr & Mrs McTavish, this letter is addressed. I hereby give you notice to vacate this croft. We have been granted permission to move all crofters so as to put this piece of land to more useful purposes. You will be given until the 24th August to vacate the croft. You must make your way to Glasgow, from where your ship will leave on the 21st September for the colony of Canada, where you shall live from now on.

Yours sincerely

James McNeill, Factor.

We all stood there, quite taken aback, just staring at each other in deathly silence. My father finally broke it.

"There must be some kind of mistake. Only yesterday McNeill was here collecting rents and he never spoke a word about it, it can't be true."

But unfortunately it was. Within two weeks we had packed all our belongings into one small wooden chest and were ready to leave. The day was grim and cloudy and our beloved islands, Rhum and Eigg, were small grey shadows in the distance, as if they had never been discovered. I took a last look at our croft, the croft MacDuigh, that had been passed down our family from generation to generation. I had to drag my brother Alasdair out, crying and hysterical, and as we departed the tiny innocent little place, I felt I had left part of me behind – my soul, which I believe is still there.

As we all left our crofts, the Mackinnons, the MacDonalds and the Stewarts, there was a deathly silence, a silence you could have cut with a knife. Then, as we walked down our long, dim glen, one person cried, then another, and before we knew it everyone was weeping long, wet, hysterical tears and every tear that dropped was like a boulder rolling and thumping the ground so hard it could have turned the whole world into turmoil.

Our journey to the mainland in small wooden boats was difficult, but we finally arrived in Mallaig port. From there we had to walk to Glasgow, which I can tell you was one treacherous journey. One particular incident springs to mind. It was just before we reached Glasgow . . .

We were walking along a dusty track. Suddenly, from out of the bushes, jumped two men. One had a knife and the other a large stick. The man with the knife. . . had black, wavy hair which was very untidy and dirty, and crawling with lice. . . He wore tweed trousers, very plain and worn. . . The man with the stick looked almost exactly the same, except that he wore a kilt with dark, murky colours, which looked like a MacDonald tartan. Before anyone could say a word, they closed in on us.

"Hand over all the money you have and we shall let you go free," announced the man with the knife.

"I have only two pounds, just enough for our ferry fare," said my father.

"I do not care. Give us the money and we will leave." My father handed them the money and both men took off up the dusty track, into their own misfortune. . .

My father looked around desperately at everyone, "We are all still living, is everyone all right?" Everyone nodded and mumbled, quite taken aback by the strange and frightening incident.

Luckily my father still had fifteen pounds, he had been lying. That night we prayed, and although he had lied, we were sure that God would find it in his heart to forgive him. . .

I remember the first time I saw our ship, the Mary Ellen. She was gigantic and her great masts soared above us, seeming to go on forever in a streamer thrown to the sky. Her sails, although tied up, were huge, and when they were let out, I was sure they would carry us to our destination.

I knew not what lay ahead in the years to come, although it filled me with promise to imagine. All I knew was that I had left Skye, the land of mist and all its wonders behind. I would never return again, never watch the great gulls that soar in the sky, never again walk the hills that kiss the clouds, and never again look out to sea and watch the grey mists closing in on the Dark Isle. As I stood there on the quay, with those thoughts engraved on my mind, I looked on with great hope and sadness; hope because of what lay ahead, and sadness for what I had left behind. So I turned to the future, where my new life awaited me. . .

HANNAH BARDELL, BROXBURN ACADEMY

THIRD PRIZE, 1996/97

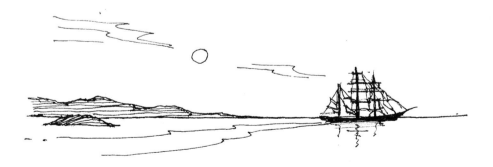

'The Clearances' they said

'Don't need you anymore' they said
'Can make profit in other ways' they said
'You have twelve hours' they said
'We'll burn your houses then' they said
'What will you have instead?' we asked
'Sheep' they said
'Make a bomb' they said
'What about us?' we asked
'You' they said
'Pack up, you're off to Australia' they said.

ANNA HOLT
JAMES GILLESPIE'S HIGH SCHOOL, EDINBURGH
COMMENDED, 1994/95

Tarik (extract)

I looked at the limp baby, and then back into his mother's frightened eyes. I knew it was dead. She knew it too, but couldn't bring herself to let it go. I held out my arms.

"Give him to me," I said gently.

Reluctantly she passed him over, taking one last look into her son's glazed eyes.

"Go back to your other child, she needs you more now," I advised. The woman walked away, glancing back now and then, but Sam had taken the baby away, to the pit.

●　　●　　●

I don't really know how I came to be out here in Bosnia. One second I had said "yes", and the next I was in a tent, seeing to people's horrifying injuries, gunshot sounding in the distance. . . The cold winter wind cut through my shoes and carried my feet off, bit by bit, to another land. I turned to Sam. "Take over for a while, will you," I said, and turned away before he could answer.

Making my way over to the tent I shared with Sam, I saw families huddled together for warmth, on the cold, hard ground. Some of them looked up at me with sorrowful eyes, and for a moment I felt like a powerful king, strolling around his kingdom. It made me feel even more guilty, guilty that I can go home to the safety of Scotland whenever I choose, like the king escaping to his luxury palace, leaving his people on the streets with nowhere to escape to. . .

I put my hand deep into my sleeping bag and pulled out a bar of chocolate, a luxury which my husband had packed for me. I didn't really think of chocolate as a luxury until I came out here.

I climbed out of the tent and stood up. The wind had become icier, and the hailstones were beginning to fall. I pulled the hood of my coat over my ears, and set off to the clump of trees just outside the camp. . .

I first heard the screams and grunts as I entered the woods. I started to run, following the sounds. In a small clearing, just one last pitiful scream rang through the air.

In the middle of the clearing a woman lay on her side. Her front bulged. I took her pulse, but it wasn't there. Silently, I made a rough grave and lifted the mother and her unborn baby in to rest, not before noticing a number branded on her forearm.

There was a rustle in the bushes. I turned sharply.

"Come out, I won't hurt you," I called.

A boy stood up. A boy of maybe nine or ten. His brown hair was tousled, his face streaked with mud. The only clothes he wore were a torn shirt and ragged trousers, three sizes too small. He had no shoes. I looked at the grave and then back at the boy.

"Was this your mother?" I asked in Serbo-Croatian. The boy looked straight at me. His big brown eyes knew too much about terror and pain, for a child.

"Yes," he said clearly, "I was to be big brother, but Mama was too exhausted."

He sat on the ground and put his hands on his forehead. He, too, had a number branded on his forearm . . .

I woke early, more from the cold than from the scarce early sunshine. Tarik was nowhere to be seen. I ran towards the trees. . . He was just placing a cross of twigs on his mother's grave. He looked up when he felt my presence behind him.

"I had to do this before I go away. I won't come back to this place, but I need to let my mother and brother know that I remembered them and will remember them always." He stood up, bowed his head in prayer, then left the clearing without looking back. I walked slowly to the grave.

"I'm sorry," I whispered, as I pulled the cross from the ground and threw it in the bushes. If a refugee found the grave, he would dig up the body and eat it. If an officer from the prison camp found it, they would know, as it was a fresh grave, that Tarik was nearby. . .

LAURA JOYCE, QUEENSFERRY HIGH SCHOOL

FIRST PRIZE (EQUAL), 1994/95

Part of this story was subsequently dramatised and performed during the Edinburgh International Festival of 1995, by a group of pupils from Bosnia, together with pupils from Queensferry High School.

Andrew

The tiniest creature
I ever saw:
a bald scalp,
crinkly skin,
small blue fingers,
stubby nails.

A precious face pictured
for my family to cherish,
never growing
and ageless,
forever the same.

My little cousin,
born dead.
No one got to know him
to look after, to love him:
departed before he arrived.

REBECCA NOBLE

CURRIE HIGH SCHOOL

COMMENDED 1997/98

I Am a Cossack

I was eight years old, but I remember everything as if it was yesterday. My father and I participated in a Cossack horse tour. I had never taken part in any trip before, and the idea of going on one, with Cossacks and horses besides, sounded fantastic! My Mother sewed me a special Cossack uniform like the one that little Cossacks used to wear: a red shirt and dark blue trousers with red stripes on trouser legs. It was my strongest desire for a long time to have such a uniform! My Father has got such trousers with red stripes, and he has also got a Cossack peaked cap, a sabre and a Cossack jacket with high collar. Our family is a Cossack family. My Father and Mother are Cossacks, and my younger sister is a Cossack too. Of course, she hasn't got trousers with stripes, but she has got a wide long skirt, and it's just her hobby to dance in front of the mirror in it. The girl!. . .

We took off from St Petersburg and we were soon in Rostov-on-Don, the capital of the Cossacks of the Don-river region. At the airport we were met by a tall black-haired man who took us to his house. . . We spent that night at his place, and the next morning a small ship brought us to a small peninsula. Our trip began.

We spent the first day in a big house in which there were many water melons, and I was eating them all day long till I nearly split my sides with overeating. Then the tall black-haired man brought us to the Don riverside. There were a lot of tents there and a lot of people in Cossack uniform. They were chattering gaily about something, and I was looking at them and thought how nice-looking and strong they were . . .

In the evening they organised a fire. I was cooking meat in a mess-tin. The Cossacks gathered near the fire, someone began to sing a song. Their choir was quite a special thing. The men's singing was long and slow, and the wind was taking the words and music down the steppe. I was sitting in the tent, looking at them and thought about the origin of these people, about the place they came from; I wondered why they called themselves 'Cossacks', and why the word 'Cossack' made them think that they were all relatives; why they were so kind to each other, why they were so proud of the words, 'I am a Cossack'. The sparks of the fire were lighting up their tanned faces, and I was imagining my ancestor Cossacks sitting near a fire many years ago, cooking meals and singing songs, ready to start marching in the morning.

When did the first Cossacks appear? Where did they come from? What are they? The steppe was their Motherland. Different people lived in the steppe at that time. Excavations show that there lived Khazars, Greeks, Romans and other peoples. It is assumed that it was exactly there in the steppe where men domesticated horses.

The word 'Cossack' existed in different languages, that is why there are so many tribal names sounding very similar to the word 'Cossack'. Scientists' opinions about where this word came from differ much. Some think that the word 'Cossack' originates from a Tatar word *goozack* which means 'free'. Still others believe that the word 'Cossack' is connected with the Turkic language and comes from a word *koz-ak* which means 'white goose'. Personally I like this version, it seems more probable to me, I often watched dancing Cossacks and often their movements reminded me of flying geese.

How did Cossacks live? In peaceful times – by hunting and fishing. Dark woods surrounded the steppe at that time. The forests were rich in wolves, foxes, deer, wild boars, ermines. Cossacks used to bring not much from the forest in order 'not to ruin a normal life of nature', but quite enough for them and their families to live on. Rivers and lakes that were numerous gave them a lot of fish: sterlets, sturgeons, different sorts of salmon, crucians, pikes, crawfish. The life of hunters made Cossacks brave and strong.

Some people think that the word 'Cossack' means a soldier on a horse with a whip in his hand (*nagajka*). It is true that Cossacks served in a cavalry troop in the Tsar's Army. But the difference between a Cossack and a common soldier was that a Cossack paid his own money for his services: he had to pay for a gun, a uniform, a horse. Due to this Cossacks never paid any taxes. Heroic deeds of a lot of Cossacks contributed much to the glorious pages of the history of Russia.

After 1917 a lot of Cossacks were killed or sent to Siberia. But many modern Cossacks remember their glorious history and they pronounce the words, 'I am a Cossack' with pride. So far, I've done nothing special, nothing that I could be proud of, but I'd like these words to be associated with something strong, nice and kind. Such were for me those people sitting around the fire on that unforgettable night and singing beautiful songs that were fading away.

At home in my desk I keep a small iron cross that was given to me in memory of that tour. When I meet anyone with a like cross I feel that we are relatives and are very close to each other, but this is not only because we were participants of that tour but also because both he and I can say, 'I am a Cossack'.

BOGDAN BORISOVICH ALMAZOV

SCHOOL NO. 328, ST PETERSBURG

HIGHLY COMMENDED, 1994/95

The Wild Horses' Charge

The horses' manes blew in the wind
Tangling, twisting, weaving.
Their tails streamed out as nature's banners
Dark, chestnut and white.

Their hooves pounded the tattoo of freedom
As they thundered over the plain.
The hard legs flew over any ground
Be it stony, grass or mud.

Their eyes rolled wild, their nostrils flared
And they leapt the dry rivers there were.
The grass grew wild and the rocks would cower
As their endless charge surged forth.

The leaders plunged to a searing halt
And the others followed suit.
The ground dropped away for thousands of feet
And the horses had no escape.

The wolves snarled, their eyes snapped
And the horses screamed in fright.
The wolves advanced, circling, waiting
For the stallion to challenge their presence.

He strode out through the mares, his head held high
And blew his challenge aloud.
The pack growled, their muscles tensed
And they sprang and cried for blood.

The stallion stormed, his screams shook the ground
And his forelegs struck out in attack.
The wolves drew back, their courage weakened
And the leader bayed for retreat.

The mares whinnied, the foals neighed
As the stallion proclaimed his victory,
His head held high, his body poised,
And the horses ran again.

LOUISE JOHNSON
ST ANDREW'S HIGH SCHOOL
KIRKCALDY
HIGHLY COMMENDED
1996/97

Football

Football, I love everything about it. Even the mention of the word seems to set off fireworks in my head. The excitement, the commitment, the passion, the feeling that you could stay absorbed in it forever. Unoriginal? Maybe, but I'd prefer to be on or at the side of a pitch than anywhere else in the world. Probably one of the most comforting aspects is the feeling that you're not alone - your obsession is shared with millions.

I walk to school with my friends on Monday morning, re-enacting goals we've seen the previous Saturday with large stones ("Here's Wallace. . . takes it past Gillon . . . passes to Gilroy . . . shoots! . . . scoooooors!!") No matter what your parent or teacher says, without football, life would just be a big, boring nil-nil draw.

But football hasn't always been a passion of mine. No, no. . . I had to learn to think and form an opinion of things first. So by the time my first football game dawned on me I must have been two or three years old. It was an unimportant game for most of the people attending, but for me everyone's eyes were on this pitch in the centre of Maryhill where Thistle and Alloa battled out a four-all draw. But my mind was on other things.

First and foremost was the dreadful pins and needles developing in my feet from being up on my dad's shoulders for so long. The other thing that intrigued me was the people: the group of older boys singing tunelessly and laughing hysterically at each other, the dirty old man behind us who kept shouting obscenities at the ref. I have a picture in my memory of him from when I turned round to look at him: his hair looked as though someone had rubbed greasy chip paper over it, his eyes were half shut and very bloodshot and his teeth were black, in contrast to his rosy red cheeks.

But the one thing they all had in common was their red and yellow hats or scarves or gloves or tops. I distinctly remember wishing I could be one of them. I was stuck with the dull black pom-pom hat, brown gloves and grey coat that my mum had wrapped me up in to keep out the winter chill.

I had to wait four years for my first taste of the real big match atmosphere. I was sitting in Ibrox, home of Glasgow Rangers. My dad had purchased two season tickets, so I was the proud owner of my very own seat. My name was engraved in a rectangular piece of metal, which was screwed onto the back of the blue plastic seat. This was a whole different world from the surroundings of Partick Thistle's humble ground.

About half-an-hour into the game something very strange happened: one minute the ground was relatively quiet, the next, the massive stadium was erupting with gleeful noise. Huge colourful flags were waved about and scarves were thrown overhead. My dad looked down at me and informed me that Rangers had scored a goal. When the shouting had eventually died down another noise took its place. Like an enormous choir the crowd rose as one and started singing. The words of this song were accompanied by clapping on every beat. I remember standing up and smiling. How could I help smiling when I was surrounded by all this happiness. When things had quietened down again I looked around at the sea of smiling faces behind me. I then realised that I was really going to like football. After all, something that made all these thousands of people happy couldn't be that bad.

Every Sunday afternoon, my friend and I walk along the main road towards Oakburn, home ground of the local football team. Fifteen minutes later, sitting in the dressing room before our game, the pre-match anxiety is at its peak. I look around at the other boys, who are looking at the manager, but I can tell that his pep-talk is going in one ear and out the other. Minds are on other things: scoring a last-minute winner from twenty-five yards, lifting the gold cup overhead, hearing the crowd roar in appreciation. But all of us know that we'll never go anywhere in football - the SYCA league third division isn't exactly renowned as a breeding ground for top quality players.

No-one is sitting still. Some boys are tapping their studs on the hard wooden floor, others are stretching against the bare stone walls. But all of our tension has disappeared by five to two. We're stripped in our team's colours ready to play. I scrutinise the opposition. They always seem to be twice as big as us and look as if they belong to a zoo rather than an Under Fourteen football team. But as the game kicks off I feel strangely important. I feel as if I'm not the spectator anymore, but the performer. And as each game passes, regardless of the score, I realise how true the immortal words of Bill Shankly are: 'Football isn't a matter of life and death - it's far more important than that'.

RODDY WALLACE

BOCLAIR ACADEMY, BEARSDEN

THIRD PRIZE, 1995/96

My Earliest Memories

Journeys to Japan and around, I remember nothing of, but I will always recall the first house my family lived in. The house was my father's parents' house, situated on the outskirts of Japan's capital, Tokyo Kawasaki.

Streets were small with cables overhead, narrow roads, and no pavements. Around the house were many blocks of grey and white flats. I always thought that the streets didn't seem to fit with each other - old houses made of wood and metal, tall opal-fruit-like buildings, and the odd drinking bar, everything was changing around us. Whenever I think of that street I can almost hear the hustle and bustle of the building constructors. . .

My grandfather was a practising doctor and had his surgery extended onto the tatty-looking house. We lived above the surgery in a two-roomed flat, where the scents of must and surgical spirit entered your nose.

. . . Two strong memories stay in my mind like glue. One is my nurse called *Kobaya-san*, who I remember playing with constantly downstairs in the surgery. My mother tells me *Kobaya-san* was one of the people who enabled me to speak Japanese from the age of three.

The second of my memories is my *obasan* (granny) and *ojisan's* (grandpa's) sitting room. In the room there were *tatamis*, (boards of woven reeds) on the floor instead of carpets. Standing on them was a deep orange

and yellow low table where we used to sit around on Japanese cushions called *zabutons*. There were inbuilt cupboards made partly out of paper and wood. The paper doors had gone slightly yellow, but despite this they seemed to look presentable. Thousands of ornaments and boxes adorned the top of the many cupboards and chests of drawers.

In one corner of the room was the family Buddhist shrine made of a carved, sombre mahogany. Every day it would be opened and *Ojisan* would strike a bowl-shaped bell to pray for his deceased relatives and ancestors. Offerings of grapes and melons would be given, often I felt not to eat the melon was unfair.

Nights usually meant getting the bulky futons out to make those well-needed beds. Bathtimes I adored, as the whole area beside the bath was waterproof. This meant I could jump out of it and wash my hair. The bath was compact, in a ghastly colour of pink, but the depth was a massive one metre at least. Again a waterproof, sealed sliding door would shut out any gushing water. Just beyond this was a washing machine, and a basin where my mother would brush my teeth. 'Lights out', but the sounds of the speeding motorbikes outside would frequently keep me awake.

In the morning when the cleaners and the rest of the house were up saying 'good morning', or '*ohiyogoziemas*' in Japanese, my mother and I often got stern looks, if not up by seven-thirty a.m.

Breakfast could be a traditional soup and a bowl of rice, but I preferred ham and egg or that worldwide favourite, cornflakes. Bread in Japan was thickly sliced and very tasty. After breakfast we often visited various small shops and a supermarket nearby.

The one problem that was a pain all through my early childhood was leaving the house. Everyone in Japan had black hair, so when my mother and I walked along the streets, we stuck out and were often approached by some silly, rude children shouting, "*Gaijin* - foreigner!" Even though I was half Japanese they spoke to me as if I spoke no Japanese. As a result, leaving the house was as stressful as staying in the house.

Apart from racism or being hassled, summer nights were the most supreme in the world. We dressed up in our quaint *yukatas* (summer style kimonos) and the temperature would be just perfect for the atmospheric festivals we enjoyed nearby. Sounds of traditional drums, folk violins, singing and dances would all be included. Held in a park, lanterns would be lit to help create a milky light, to see the many stalls at the side selling toys, and all things called enjoyment. One of my favourite stalls was the water balloon yo-yo stall, where balloons would be filled with water and made into a yo-yo. The smells of rubber and water seemed to merge, and stay imprinted on my mind. The evening would most definitely be rounded off with an ancient Japanese folk dance, as hundreds gathered round to join one another in unison. Everybody would carnival the night away, as the warm, slow southern wind blew through my hair.

When I actually sit back, analyse, write and think, I would say it was an interesting experience. The cultural differences, language, manners, all have influenced me in one way or another. Compared with a child in this country, I feel my earliest memories are unconventional, but yet in my view they have made me think in a better, much broader way about life.

EMILY OYAMA, THE ROYAL HIGH SCHOOL, EDINBURGH

FIRST PRIZE (EQUAL), 1995/96

Poems in the
Style of Japanese Tanka

THE CHERRY'S BLOSSOM
When cherries blossom
They are related to clouds.
Maybe that's why
Soul becomes as wide
As the blue sky in spring.

●　　●　　●

THE SUMMER MOON
It's summer's night.
Mountainsides are hidden
Thickly by branches of leaves.
Even the shining moon
Fades under shades of trees

●　　●　　●

THE AUTUMN STORM

Fierce Autumn storm
Breaks off the leaves of the trees
And today for the first time
I remember in grief
The beauty of autumn garden

●　●　●

THE ENDLESS RAIN

Rain has no end
All the bamboo leaves fell.
They hid from friends
Narrow mountain path.
None of my friends come to me.

●　●　●

THE WINTER MOON

It's seemed to the pilgrim as though
wonderful spangles of moon
Fly from the sky to the Earth
While snow falls at night
to the pilgrim's clothes

ALLA BOGOMOLOVA, SCHOOL NO.295, ST PETERSBURG

HIGHLY COMMENDED, 1996/97

The Ballerina (extract)

On top of Amy's cupboard, acting as a bookstop on the bookcase, stood a musical box. It was a beautiful musical box, shiny black, with flowery, golden patterns on the lid. It was closed, and on the lid stood a ballerina.

She was wearing a frilled tutu and an elegant leotard. One hand she held behind her, closed loosely on the edge of her tutu, the other was bent before her face. In this hand she clasped a spray of flowers, and her head was bent gracefully over them, as if to catch their sweet fragrance. Her left toe was pointed in front of her, and her right leg was slightly bent behind. Her poise was perfect, her position sure and confident. She was made of steel.

Beautifully graceful and perfect though her position was, so that one would hardly want it to change, there was a certain 'fixedness' about it. That curved arm flowed from the shoulder to the tips of the fingers with unmoving movement, but it would never lift from the tutu. That bent leg looked just about to straighten, but it was fixed so for ever. Those eyes would never gaze at anything but that colourless spray of flowers in that grey, steel hand. One almost wondered: 'What good does this ballerina do if her only dance is the dance of the light upon the metal? What good are those flowers if they will never delight anyone with colour or a sweet aroma? What good is that silver face if it will never be anything but immovable steel?'

The ballerina felt this too, in her cold steel heart. Secretly she longed to be able to dance and delight people like a real ballerina. But that could never happen, could it?. . .

●　　●　　●

The family was to go and see a performance of the ballet *The Sleeping Beauty* very soon and the house was agog with excitement. As Amy commented: "What with Kirsten's ballet exam, and now this, we seem to be doing a lot of ballet at the moment!"

When the day came, Amy's little brother, Nathan, grabbed the steel ballerina at the last minute, saying, "I want to show her to the ballerinas!"

He was only a very little boy.

So, in the big theatre, packed with people rustling bags and talking in the dark, the three children sat, impatient for the show to begin. And the steel ballerina watched from her seat in a bag, squashed between two muslins and a bottle of orange squash.

The curtain rose. The orchestra began to play, and the dancers, professional ballet dancers, took up the dance.

What was the piano compared with an orchestra of professional musicians, all their many different instruments combining to make the wondrous sounds of Tchaikowsky's music? What was one small grade three girl, Amy's little sister Kirsten, to many, many beautiful ballet dancers, all long past grade eight? You did not need to have an eye for beauty to recognise that dancing for what it was: true ballet, graceful, and spiced with the enjoyment of those who took part in it, lifted or dropped by the music that followed it everywhere, like a boat sailing on the waves of the sea.

The steel ballerina watched with a weeping heart the real, wonderful warmth and colour and movement on the stage, and knew herself to be cold and grey and fixed forever. And could she have done so she would have wept . . .

AMY TODD, KINROSS HIGH SCHOOL

FIRST PRIZE, 1997/98

Poem

Railways, like bandage,
Tie up the mummy of England.
Wineglass of red-eyed Sangria
Is trembling in frozen hands.
The train rushes towards the sunset. . .
My shadow slides across the wall. . .
Leaves are scratching at the window
Of compartment with twinkling lamp.
Beyond the glass – the dove-grey hills,
Like scrawny shoulders. . .
Under the sandal of the train
English evening dies. . .
Sheep grey-haired as stones,
Are scattered all over the clover.
Haggard peacock is snoring,
Sleeping on the tree.
Asexual attendant has brought
The cup of British tea.
Paper clouds only for me
Seem to be faces of the dead.
From the grey-eyed cup
I swallow the moon's reflection.
Beyond the blank-eyed glass
My feeble-voiced dreams gleam.
They say, angels,
As ancient sculptures,
Have no pupils in their eyes.
They say, blind angels
Are everywhere around me.

So, turning the light off,
I lie down in the blank-eyed night.
And hundreds of angels' eyes
With blind unpupilled gaze
Promise to me that the whole
Night they'll be with me. . .
Blank-eyed souls again
Are looking for me.
Blank mouths keep silent,
Drinking my wine.
I am sleeping in a
        blank-eyed dream,
I am going mad bit by bit. . .
And the train rushes
Towards the dawn. . .
And my shadow
Sleeps on the wall.

DARIA BELOVA
SCHOOL NO.195, ST PETERSBURG
FIRST PRIZE, 1997/98

[83]

Ghost Train

The story starts with Kirsti dashing for the 18.45 train at Waverley station. She notices that the train is one of the old ones, rather dusty and musty. Tired out, she falls asleep, only wakening as the train pulls into her station, Dalmeny. But everything seems oddly changed. . .

. . . I was just about to start off down the hill, when a guard came running up.

"Hoi, missy!. Do you have a ticket for that train?"

"No, but I've got the money," I replied, extending the change from my pocket. He counted it, then gave me a suspicious look. He was holding up a brand new 50p coin.

"What's this, then?" he asked, glaring at me. "Some kind of joke?"

"No, "I repled, mystified. "It's just a 50 pence piece."

"Do you really expect me to believe this is a normal coin?" he shouted, pointing at it. "1997, it says. You can't have a 1997 coin!"

"But. . . " I started, then realised it was pointless to argue. "There!" I said, handing him a sticky pound coin. The cross guard . . . finally gave me a ticket.

. . . As I walked on past the collection of shops near Lover's Lane, I was surprised to see Mr Todger's Carpets and Keys, formerly a grocery, had reverted to selling food again! I was even more surprised to see that Mrs Todger, who had died of cancer in 1994, was serving at the counter. It couldn't possibly be her! She was dead and buried, I had seen her grave. I walked over to get a closer look - surely it was Mrs Todger! It was so like her!

Puzzled, I continued up the hill to the square I lived in . . . Walking up my own garden path, I said "Hello" to our neighbour, Sheila Dunnett, but she just looked round as if she did not know who had spoken. I stopped in surprise at the front door, when I realised it was not its usual green, but yellow! I harked back to my early childhood - before it was green it was red, and before it was red, it was . . . it was . . . I struggled to remember - yellow! I shook my head in disbelief. This was a strange day!

As I knocked at the door, a furry tail rubbed against my legs. "Hello, puss," I said, scratching its ears. It reminded me of a cat I'd had when I was younger. Bunter was his name. The door opened and my Mum's voice called out: "Bunter, teatime!" I was so shocked, I nearly fell backwards off the step. A woman of about 30 stood in the doorway, her long brown hair lying loose over her cotton top. She was wearing a long Indian skirt which billowed in the wind as she called in the cat. This was my mother, I was certain, but she looked so much younger!

"Er, hello, Mum," I said, not sure what to say. She looked puzzled.

"Hello, who's there?" she called, peering round.

"Me!" I cried, but she didn't seem to hear. What was going on? Things were so mixed up - the train bridge, the school, Mrs Todger, the door, Bunter. As my mother looked round, I brushed past her into the hall. . . Then I heard the unmistakable sound of a baby crying. "Just coming, Kirsti!" shouted my mother, as she bustled past me through the kitchen to the living room. With a feeling of dread, I walked slowly through the kitchen. There were no nice new cupboards, the table was not the usual magnificent pine, but cheap and grey, the chairs a scrappy mixture. . . This was what it had looked like when I was three, I realised with a shock. More crying came from the living-room, and I moved nervously forward to get a look at the child.

Short, ginger hair framed a very slightly freckled face. I stared, and blue-green eyes stared back. The baby was, it was . . . me!

"No!" I screamed, "This is a nightmare!"

The baby started to cry again, and an unpleasant odour wafted into the air.

"Oh!" said my mother, and disappeared upstairs . . . When she came back with a white cloth and several safety pins, I felt my stomach lurch. That was me, I thought in scornful disgust. The same person who got 1s on her report cards and had never (yet) failed a test, was now lying on the floor getting her nappy changed? This was an outrage, I shouldn't be seeing it! I ran out of the room and up the stairs to the refuge of my bedroom . . . to try to put the confusion out of my mind. But I stopped in surprise and horror - no bed was in the room, just a wooden cot!

"Aaaaarghhh!!!" I screamed. The room began to spin crazily, until all went black and I knew no more. . .

I half-opened my eyes. All around me I saw the anxious faces of my family.

"What happened?" asked my mother.

"Where have you been?" My brother's freckled face loomed overhead.

"How long have you been here?" said my father, frowning at me in concern?

I groaned, squinting in the light."I don't know, I don't know," I murmured. . . It took me a while to remember, then it all came flooding back, and I poured out my story to the confused members of my family.

"Are you sure?" asked Dad

"Must have been that bump on the head," said my brother, with a knowing wink.

Just then I glanced at the clock - 11 o'clock! I jumped up.

"Have I been asleep four hours?" I spluttered.

"I don't know," my mother said. "We just heard you cry out."

I sat back, puzzled. . . "I got on the train alright," I said, still confused. My parents looked at each other.

"When you were late, we called the station and they said the 18.45 never ran."

I sighed. It had been a really weird day. Just then I felt the crinkle of paper in my pocket. It was the ticket the guard had given me. I was about to throw it away, when I noticed the date stamped on it - 17th August 19...**84**

KIRSTI MCGREGOR

QUEENSFERRY HIGH SCHOOL

HIGHLY COMMENDED, 1997/98

Benefactor Thief

Seema was going along the road, walking round the puddles left over by the recent cold autumn rain. She looked downcast. Everything was bad. The quarrel with her friend, the rudeness of the chief . . . and that was not all. There were two days till her salary and buying some food, which was in her bag, had required half the money she had. And it was necessary to repair her shoes which were absolutely torn. She felt cold and it was horrible that she could not get home, because she had lost her key and had to wait for her son to come back from technical school. He may also need some money. She imagined what she looked like: it was not a pleasant sight. Who would notice that she had a nice pretty face and slim figure, beautiful hair? . . .

Seema stopped near a shop window to have a look at herself. She looked up . . . Oh, how cruel and merciless her fate was! She saw the dummy behind the glass with a mink fur coat on its shoulders. In the dummy's hand there was such a price ticket that Seema didn't even dare to read. And . . .

there was a reflection of herself near the splendid fur coat, as if in contrast. Seema could not even dream of such a coat. And still she wanted to have a closer look at it. So she entered the shop.

"What can I do for you, Madam?" the assistant asked Seema with exaggerated politeness. Seema blushed. It seemed to her that the sales girl eyed her from top to toe with scorn, hardly keeping down her ironical smile.

"Well?" thought Seema and trying to sound natural asked, "May I try this coat on?"

The assistant eyed Seema again and after a short pause said: "It is just your size," and giving Seema the fur coat she pointed at the mirror. "Here you are."

Seema left her coat and bag on the chair, put on the fur coat, looked in the mirror and stood stunned: a beautiful queen looked at her out of the mirror. The dark brown fluffy fur sparkled under the lights and Seema's golden hair on the fur gave unusual charm to her beauty.

"Nicely done and just for you!" the sales girl said. "And it becomes you. You look splendid!"

Seema knew that it was a rare case when a woman could pay a compliment to another woman. She looked in the mirror trying to remember for her whole life the reflection of the queen she would never see again: Cinderella would have to take off the princess's attire and return from the fairy to the grey life, the life counting every penny, the life full of everyday worries and misfortunes.

Besides Seema had to think what she would say returning the fur coat: she could not confess that she had no money like that, and that she wanted to forget about all problems and feel herself a queen. Maybe she would ask the assistant to write out the bill and say she wanted to return home for the money. And then she would never appear near this shop. . .

"Excuse me, Ma'am, you are of course going to take this beautiful fur coat, but I have excellent Italian high boots which would look fine with it. Would you try them on?" Seema turned: there was a young man in front of her with a pretty box in his hands with a foreign label on it.

"Try them on, it won't harm you," he went on, opening the box, "and they are not expensive, only one-twentieth of this fur coat price."

Seema looked at him and then dropped her eyes to her own shoes and gave a glance to Italian high boots.

"I wonder, if I ask this fellow to write out a bill too?" she thought." But the high boots are very good indeed. If to be a queen – then to be a complete queen. I shall try them on then return them, saying that they hurt my heel."

Seema sat down at the edge of a chair, took off her shoes and put them in her bag quickly so as not to give the man an opportunity to notice that the welt had come unstuck. Then she pulled on the high boots. . . No, miracles never come alone! The high boots did not hurt her heel, they were the right size and very comfortable. And how they suited the fur coat!

Seema looked in the mirror and could not tear her glance away. But moments of happiness are too short, she might not delay more, so unwillingly she took off the fur coat.

"I am going to take it," Seema said to the sales girl, licking her dry lips, "write out the bill, please."

She extended her hand for the bag . . . but her fingers felt only the cold seat of the chair.

"My bag!" she cried hoarsely. "Oh, heavens! What rogues they are!" Seema sobbed breathlessly, she wished to cry. And it was not the money that Seema thought about, it was not the bag itself although it was the only one. As a matter of fact there were her shoes in her bag. She had not any shoes to wear in winter. She had to give the high boots back but what would she do then? Splash through the cold puddles in stockings only? . . .

Seema rose, her eyes expecting to meet the sympathetic, but adamant eyes of the owner of the high boots. . . There was the sales girl's face in front of her, and, faltering, she babbled:

"Oh, you poor thing! What a terrible accident! That is my fault, I did not take proper care! Oh, I am so sorry! I might have guessed that he gave those high boots to you on purpose in order to distract you, and to steal your bag where you had the money for the fur coat. Let us call the police!"

Seema glanced around: there was no owner of the high boots to be seen. Seema stopped crying and biting her lips, shook her head and ran to the exit.

. . . Seema was going home, walking round the puddles left over by the recent cold autumn rain, trying not to spoil the Italian high boots. The fairy has finished, but unlike the real fairytale, this Cinderella left the king's palace, not in the princess's dress, but she had both cut-glass shoes on her feet.

Seema walked trying to imagine to herself how the owner of the high boots was running, trying to be as far as he could from that shop. He would hide in a corner and dip his hand into her bag looking forward to how the money intended for the fur coat would rustle in his fingers. . . but coming up against the carton of milk. Seema tried to imagine the expression on his face, when he at last understood his mistake. But that was beyond her imagination: her imagination was exhausted.

VLADLENA SAMTELADZE

HIGH SCHOOL OF GLOBAL EDUCATION NO.631, ST PETERSBURG

FIRST PRIZE, 1993/94

The Lion

Muckle heid,
Jaggy yellae teeth,
Slavers dark wae blood.

Lang strang shooders,
Tail ahint, tense an soople lik a snake,
Pits his fit an the jungle flair an the braid palm leaves chitter,
But his paw breks nae deid bird's banes.

He flits,
Sleekit an still lik a warlock's shadda.

Loups lik a shark wae its blood burnin,
An wae a skelp o yellae teeth, the ragdoll deer coups tae the grund
wae a crash o banes.

Athoot keekin back, he donners aff,
The braid palm leaves chitter!

LEANNE BROWN

BIGGAR HIGH SCHOOL. THIRD PRIZE

AND SPECIAL PRIZE FOR AN ENTRY IN THE SCOTS LANGUAGE, 1997/98

Nan

It was a dark, windy night. Rain billowed like the sails of a ship against the trees. The trees themselves seemed to be alive. Great branches like arms reached out and clawed at the midnight sky. The wind whistled and shrieked across the surrounding countryside, making the huge dark clouds travel swiftly across the sky, covering and uncovering the pale sliver of moon.

The girl ran. The trees clawed at her hair, her clothes, her body. Long, thin, fingerlike branches. And all the time the wind seemed to be screeching her name. "Nan!" it hissed, "Nan!"

Nan raised a hand to her wet face, to wipe unshed tears from her eyes, eyes half shut because of the force of the wind and the rain, which beat against her face like grit. She was out of breath. Her long hair wrapped itself around her face, blowing in all directions. She pulled it away, but she didn't slow her stumbling, awkward run.

Suddenly it was not these elements, but the uneven earth that hit her as she fell in a headlong tumble of hair and rain and feet and arms and whispering wind.

"Nan! Hurry up wi thon washin. We've no got a day tae get it finished" . . . Nan pretended not to hear. The water in the tub was growing cold and her wet hands were freezing.

"Ah'll no be like her. Ah'll no be like her." And Nan thought to herself, with a small, secret smile, "There's awayis the nicht tae look forward tae."

They'd all met. The storm which had huffed and puffed that afternoon had calmed to a slight breeze. The sky was clear. Nan was excited.

When she arrived things were already well under way. Dancers twirled and swirled and the bagpipes dirled. The candles flickered and the night was alive with the shouts and shrieks of the dancers. As a group neared her, their hands parted and she was hauled in. Now she was dancing with them. They spun in a circle, faster and faster, until everything was a

blur of light and laughter and music and heat.

When the dance was over, the lively music began again and a new dance was started. Before she joined another group, Nan glanced around at her companions, all with shining faces, and smiled happily at the Guest of Honour sitting in the corner, playing a quick, lively jig on the bagpipes.

That evening, Nan had worn her best dress. But after an hour or so of dancing, she was so hot. She looked around at the other dancers. Some of them had already removed garments.

"Och, naebiddy even minds," she said to herself, as she did the same. She joined another dance, feeling much better, and soon she was lost in the music and the laughter and the heat and the light once more.

He had ruined it with a drunken shout. He had tried to put an end to her hopes and dreams. The dancing had stopped, the music had stopped and all had gone dark. In a great rush of embarrassment and humiliation and anger, she had pursued him, the others at her heels, as the storm rose again.

She wiped mud from the side of her face and from her mouth. She dragged herself to her feet and ran on after him, determined to catch him this time and to show the shrieking crowd that she was as good as them.

The rain was still falling, but the wind had died down. The voices that had been calling her name were silent now. Her petticoat was sodden, and her hair dirty and matted. In her filthy hand, his horse's grey tail dangled. She turned to her fellow witches and laughed triumphantly.

HANNAH GRAY, BEESLACK HIGH SCHOOL, PENICUIK

HIGHLY COMMENDED, 1997/98

Jess

my cat is witless,
and rather plump –
but she has certain capabilities.

she can open doors,
and climb trees
and make judicious displays
of affection.

she knows the cosiest places
to sleep,
and that the tin-opener
is her best friend.

I am not so limited, or so I like to think,
and I have more articulate ways
of expressing my emotions
than rolling over on the ground.

yet poetry remains
an unyielding cat-flap.
I don't understand why it is spaced out funny on the
page like

t

    h

      i

        s

MARION SIMPSON

CLEVEDEN HIGH SCHOOL, GLASGOW

FIRST PRIZE, 1993/94

Dust - Gatherers (abridged)

Every so often, as I move between stale-smelling racks of books, china and second-hand clothes, I feel a certain revulsion. I am tired of re-arranging, sorting and labelling these objects, which, however tasteless, will find a buyer; our customers never stop to think whether a thing will be used, or whether it will just sit on a mantelpiece, gathering dust, until it comes back to us so that someone else may let it gather dust in their house for another few decades.

My musings along these lines were focused on a lime-green velvet jacket with the most hideous yellow fastenings I had ever seen, when I had to go over to the door to collect a fusty bag of old curtains. When I turned my attention again to the lime-green jacket, I saw that it had fallen to the ground. As I picked it up, I noticed that it was unnaturally heavy, so, curious, I looked inside the pockets. To my great surprise and interest, I found an old pocket-watch, probably silver, I thought, although it was so dirty that I couldn't tell. There was also a piece of paper which looked like a tram car ticket, and, though it was faded and unclear, I could just about make out the date: 12th March - or was it May? - 1938. I remember that the watch happened to be at the right time, even though it obviously hadn't been wound for many years.

In the shop, we have a procedure for dealing with valuable finds, and I marched proudly into the room with 'Private - Authorised Personnel Only' on the door. Joyce's office has one of those glass windows through which she can see the shop without being seen . . .

"Miriam Stenhouse," she announced in her hoarse, gravelly voice. "That's who it was that handed the jacket in, so that's who this watch belongs to. Do you know who that is?" In my mind, I ran over faces of our customers, trying to remember if there was anyone who could possibly have owned something so tasteless as that jacket. But I could not, and shook my head. "Listen, why don't you take it round to old Mrs Stenhouse's flat? She'd be pleased to see you if she's lost this, and I've got her address." . . .

'Philip Stenhouse' was the inscription on the door, but my knock was answered by a small, well-dressed, elderly woman whom I recognised as one of our regular customers. A dainty smile lit up her face, and a remembered remark flashed through my mind: Mrs Stenhouse had once boasted to Joyce that her doctor had called her 'the most feminine woman of eighty-three he had in his practice'.

"You're the little girl from the charity shop, aren't you, dear?" she asked, and I nodded. She would not let me explain my purpose over the threshold, and invited me in, promptly offering me a cup of tea. Feeling rather flustered, I accepted, and she ushered me into her living room. I sat down on the edge of her spotless chintz settee and surveyed the room as I waited uneasily. Against one wall was a wooden cabinet containing well-polished silver and assorted china miniatures, and over beside the window was a Bechstein concert grand piano, free of dust and the keys sparkling as they caught light from outside. There was a small set of bookshelves enclosed in a glass cupboard - that, too, was clean - and a collection of identically-bound books arranged inside. One thing especially caught my eye; in one corner was a case of military medals and decorations, mounted on a regal background of purple velvet. I became yet more curious when I noticed in this display a watch similar to the one I had found in the pocket of the lime-green velvet creation. Next to it was an empty space, as if reserved for something she had yet to obtain.

At that moment, she brought into the room a tray bearing two bone china cups resting on delicate saucers, with a matching milk jug covered in something which I believe you call a showercloth - a patch of lace trimmed with coloured beads. She sat down on an armchair opposite me, and handed me a cup of tea. In retrospect, I am still not sure why, but, in this elegant and foreign environment, I was becoming increasingly flustered and troubled, and it was probably this which made me drop the cup. My right leg and her beige carpet were soaked in hot tea (it was fortunate for the carpet, if not for my leg, that I had taken no milk) and the cup lay shattered on the floor.

At this point, the woman's reaction puzzled me; I expected her to be angry, or at the very least upset, but she remained calm, inquiring kindly for my leg, and assuring me that the cup was "only another thing, gathering dust in the kitchen." Her talk of dust-gatherers then reminded me of my purpose in visiting her, and I produced the watch from my polythene bag. Miriam Stenhouse's face showed first puzzlement, then recognition, finally joy, as if she had been re-united with a dear friend after many long years of separation, and I saw her eyes fill with tears as she reached out her frail, delicate hand towards me. She opened the casing, examined the watch face until she seemed sure that it was hers, and began to weep. I thought it best to let her cry; her tears were not tears of extreme sadness, regret, or worry, but of nostalgia and sentiment.

I felt increasingly awkward, and I wanted to leave, although I could not see how. She raised her head and looked at me, as if she was only then realising my presence. Then she spoke in a choking voice:

"Oh, my dear, I'm most terribly, terribly sorry - I'm being most impolite. Do forgive me!" Composing herself, she continued. "You see, dear, my father gave me this watch. It was in 1938, just before the war. I remember it so clearly: he was just about to take the boat back to Hamburg, and I think he must have known that I wouldn't see him again. Look – in this case over here – I have his decorations from the First World War. 'Hermann Goldstein - Captain', it says. He was a very brave man – my brother Leo, too. This is his watch here in the case. You see, it is just like mine – a little bigger, perhaps, and I keep it polished. He was killed in the First World War, Leo, before I came over here. And these pieces are all I have left of them both."

Awkwardly, I stammered that I was glad I had brought back something which was obviously so important to her, and she smiled tearfully. As I turned to leave, however, she stopped me.

"Excuse me, dear, but I'd like you to have this watch." I could not believe my ears, and began to protest, but she cut me short. "I suppose it was intended that I should give this to one of my children, but I never had any. I am old now, and, when I die, all these things will be sold since my family are all dead. You see, I don't want this watch to be sold, and I want you to have it. And, when you use it, I'd like you to think of Miriam Goldstein."

I still felt uneasy, but I took the watch anyhow, because she had given it to me. She made me promise to come back and see her, but as it happened, she became ill shortly afterwards, and I never heard the stories which she would probably have told me about her childhood and her years in Glasgow before the war. Now the watch sits here on the table beside me, and when I look at it, I think about Hermann Goldstein taking the boat back to Hamburg and to death. I think about Leo Goldstein, and how he died in battle, and I think about Miriam, and how she gave me her watch so that someone else could share the stories of her life. I like to think that the watch gathers memories as well as dust.

MARION SIMPSON

CLEVEDEN SECONDARY SCHOOL, GLASGOW

FIRST PRIZE, 1993/94

Anger by a Piano

Anger is not a musician.
That's obvious
as I thud out the music.
The sweetness
of Grechanionov's *Mazurka*
and Merkel's *Children's March*
is lost in a great tidal wave
of hatred and pain.
The pain that is left after betrayal.
Dvorak's *Largo from the New World Symphony*
no longer seems a homely, broad tune
when played with flats and sharps
in all the wrong places.
And only I could make
Offenbach's *Can-Can*
into a hateful, joyless theme.
Beethoven's *Moonlight Sonata*
falls to pieces when played
Staccato rather than
Legato.
But who really cares?
I think
as I pierce and prod
more distorted chords.

From a distance,
She is a confused
Jewish child,
Her brow furrowed in concentration,
and her large,
brown eyes reflecting
In the darkness of my piano.

RACHEL NATANSON, WEBSTER'S HIGH SCHOOL

KIRRIEMUIR

HIGHLY COMMENDED, 1994/95

Lessons of Music

She was quite different three years ago . . . She would open the door and say, laughing gaily: "Well, maestro, we haven't caught up with Svyatoslav Richter yet . . . And you are sitting incorrectly. Your legs are too short to get to the floor. So you have to use a small bench . . . There is no music without support." She would laugh loudly, turning all my mistakes into a joke, and I used to think that playing the piano was no problem at all.

Sometimes her husband would come to pick her up. He was a lively, broad-shouldered, loud-voiced man. They would run with a hop, skip and a jump downstairs towards their car, where Bobby was waiting for them. "A real Englishman, he is!" my teacher would say, "a real thoroughbred. I sewed him a tartan overcoat, trousers and a cap . . . Just look at him! A real lord, he is!" And Bobby would behave like a real lord, trotting on the lead proudly ahead of his master. Sometimes he would look back at them as if inviting everybody to admire them, so well-proportioned, so youthful looking, so smart and strong. His master and mistress would follow him, laughing and talking gaily . . .

Before the summer holidays we had a farewell party celebrating a school year end and drinking a traditional tea. . . My mother picked me up earlier than usual.

"Your teacher's husband is very ill," my mum said. "These are hard times for her."

When I came back after the holidays I heard from a distance the sounds of a Chopin waltz coming from our classroom. The waltz seemed to be so sad that I felt a lump in my throat. I opened the door gently.

My teacher was sitting at the piano, her eyes closed, moving in time to the music. It shocked me that she looked twenty years older. With grey hair, a dark kerchief on her shoulders, she looked like a big, sad bird. Just near the threshold there was Bobby, who didn't jump or bark, he just glanced at me with his sad, watery eyes. I understood that my teacher's husband had died.

Since that time, the music lessons that I loved so much changed greatly. My teacher hardly ever smiled, she always seemed to be thinking about something of her own, working with me mechanically. When I played well she just looked out of the window, when I failed some runs, she just showed me my mistakes as if I was not alive. I recollected the time when every mistake was turned into a joke, but now. . . As if I was talking to an exercise book.

Bobby never came to school again. Before the New Year concert my teacher didn't come to school either. She didn't call up, didn't warn anybody . . . The concert that used to be a real holiday for everybody, with all its excitement, flowers and tea-drinking ceremony, in the end was just a failure . . .

I dared to ring her up. Nobody answered. I rang her every day, and got her at last.

"Oh, it's you," she said and laughed strangely. "Just as I was thinking that nobody needs me . . . Bobby got under a car . . . " and she started crying. "That's it! I've got nobody now, and I'm just an old woman."

She really got old. She got a habit to muffle herself up in a kerchief, to rub her hands as if she was constantly freezing. She stayed in the classroom after lessons. Sometimes I stood in the corridor listening to her going round the room or playing some sad pieces. I could hardly keep from crying. I didn't know what to do to make her as gay as she used to be, to be my former teacher. She started reading some strange books about incarnation of souls. These black books lay on the piano like black stones.

Her pupils left her for other teachers, because she didn't really teach them any longer. We just went over pieces we had already learned.

Spring came. My teacher used to like working in her small garden in the country, and there used to be all sorts of seedlings on the window-sill in our classroom: future beautiful flowers, cucumbers, tomatoes . . . There was nothing like that this year. When I brought in some budding poplar twigs she just breathed in their smell and said: "I should go to my country home some day. Yes, during the spring holidays. Haven't been there for a year."

We didn't' see her for two weeks, but when I came back to school after the holidays I could hardly recognize her.

"Oh God!" she said. "If only you knew what had happened." She was energetically going round the classroom, speaking loudly and gesticulating. I had almost forgotten when she had last looked like this.

"Do you remember, you brought those poplar twigs? Oh, that smell! . . . I couldn't help going to the country. Alone for the first time. And I worked a lot, and so fruitfully. Got tired. Stayed there for a night. And you won't believe it, I saw my husband and Bobby in my dream! They were so gay and young. My husband gives me Bobby and is laughing . . . I woke up and thought . . . Bobby, he was gone, too . . . Started crying . . . But in the morning when I opened the door, suddenly . . . well . . . a small doggie on the porch. You won't believe. An exact replica of Bobby, only a female. And she

cried bitterly asking me to hold her in my arms . . . And I see it's somebody's dog, lost and hungry. I washed her, gave her some food . . . It was as if she had been living with me . . . But it was somebody else's dog. So I took her and went to find her owners.

They were a young couple. he is a sailor, she is a model. God knows what they had bought a doggie for. Nobody cared for her . . . I said: 'I would like to buy the dog, but I don't have enough money.' And the doggie just sat in front of me, looking at me, looking. So I decided to buy her whatever the price should be! . . . But her master, the sailor, smiled and said: 'Well, you take her. Without money. I see you've made friends already. We can't look after her.'. . . Just happiness! We are sitting here and she is waiting for me there. Missing me! I must hurry! . . . Well, let's start with arpeggios. Oh my! What do we have here instead of fingers? Italian spaghetti, yes, we do . . ."

She was the same as she used to be.

After the lesson she hugged me and said: "My husband sent me Jemma, for me not to get crazy. Bobby's soul is in her now. Do you believe in reincarnation?"

I belong to the Orthodox Church and don't believe in any reincarnation, but I know that a person cannot be alone. There must be someone who would love you! And there must be someone whom you would love, even if it's not a human soul but just a dog!

"It's nice that Jemma is a female. So she'll have puppies! I'll give you a pup," she said, powdering her nose and putting on her hat with a movement I had almost forgotten. "Agree?"

Yes, I agree, but what will my parents say?

(P.S. This story is based on real facts.)

BOGDAN BORISOVICH ALMAZOV

SCHOOL NO.328, ST PETERSBURG

FIRST PRIZE, 1995/96

The Ballad of Kezzie

After the story by Theresa Breslin

Kezzie's Father lived in Stonevale
A miner to his trade
Kezzie, Lucy and Granddad John
A family proud they made.

Disaster struck one lovely day
As down the pit they worked
Pit props collapsed, they trapped the men
And several men were hurt.

Kezzie's father bravely went back
Before it was too late
He dragged the broken props aside
To save them from their fate.

The men were saved but he was lost
Upon that fateful day
A family sad he left behind
As he was ta'en away.

Although he was a well liked man
Not many came to grieve
So saddened Kezzie soon found out
Her house she'd hae to leave.

The factor came and threw them out
Into the streets they fled
A kindly farmer helped them out
To a bothy he them led.

Money was short, the life was hard
But Kezzie saved the day
Potato picking pulled them thru'
And helped them on their way.

Winter drew near, tatties ran out
'Nae food without nae pay'
Rabbits and veg brought round by Matt
The winter held at bay.

Work in the local factory
No more work on the land
Things seemed to be getting better
Until fate took a hand.

Now injured in an accident
Kezzie did not come back home
Her sister hunted hi' and lo'
And far and wide did roam.

Searching through the streets of Glasgow
Found lost and all alone
They shipped her off to Canada
There to make a new home.

Kezzie returned, sister was gone
Some money she must find
On Canada she set her sight
Her land she left behind.

Kezzie made friends where e'er she went
Helped all along the way
At last she found her sister dear
So ill she had to stay.

For months she hovered at death's door
Until her friend they found
Then safe at last, they homeward went
To Scotland they were bound.

CHRISTOPHER WINDMILL
BEATH HIGH SCHOOL
COMMENDED, 1997/98

Quiver

She didn't deserve this but never complained,
As she clutched on to her oxygen mask, her angelic face shining
through,
eyes smiling.
Steadily the machine, holding her to life,
Kept up its insistent rhythm
Inhale   Quiver   Woosh
Inhale   Quiver   Woosh

What was she thinking?
Did the machine remind her of the music of her first dance?
Did its rhythm remind her of her sewing machine
Busily working for her family?
Or was she thinking of the next stage in life?
Death.
Heaven?
Steadily the machine, holding her to life
kept up its insistent rhythm
Inhale   Quiver   Woosh

Gripping her daughter's hand, linking her with life
She couldn't' speak but her eyes watched, smiling her love.
Inhale   Quiver   Woosh
Inhale   Quiver   Woosh

Suddenly the machine seemed to stutter.
She pressed the mask harder to her face.
Her daughter's hand slipped out of hers.
Unsteadily the machine tried to hold her to life
Kept up its uncertain rhythm
Inhale   Quiver Woosh
Inhale   Quiver   Woosh

We watched, transfixed, the movements round her bed
Doctors and nurses emerged from every corner
White coats flapping, faces expressionless.
The curtains were drawn
And now the only thing linking us with her life
Was the noise of the machine
Inhale   Quiver Woosh
Inhale   Quiver   Woosh

What did she sense now?
Did she see the nurses and doctors swarming around her?
Were their swirling coats her first dancing partners?
Or shirts tumbling from her sewing machine?
Or were they the angels already awaiting her?
The curtain gave one final flutter.
We waited, listening, dreading.
Inhale   Quiver   Woosh
                            Inhale Quiver Woosh
Inhale   Quiver   Woosh
Inhale . . .

ROB MCLAREN

PERTH ACADEMY

THIRD PRIZE, 1994/95

Dear Diary: the Homecoming

This story is based on the tragic fate of the Iolaire, the vessel that sank early on 1 January 1919, just outside Stornoway harbour, drowning many soldiers who had survived the First World War, only to die within sight of home.

Dec. 27th

So many people I know got that dreaded telegram . . . poor wives and mothers who will never see their loved ones again. They must be heartbroken. There's a young girl, Peggy, in our own village here, who's lost her husband and her wee boy is just Catriona's age. I can't imagine how she must be feeling . . . I bumped into her earlier today. I stopped to speak to her, and suddenly she burst into tears right in front of me. I took her back home and made her a cup of tea. She told me how much she was missing her husband, and how no-one seemed to offer her any sympathy now, they were all so excited about the boat coming. I felt really guilty. Here I am getting ready for the homecoming, and there she is feeling so alone and sad.

Dec. 30th

Only two more days! I hardly got a wink of sleep last night just thinking about it . . . all the good times we had together and all the good times we will have in the future. I've got the iron heating to press the few clothes he left behind, and I must bake some bread too. Catriona looks at me as if I were mad! We looked at Calum's photos together. He looks so handsome with his lovely blond hair and clean-shaven face; his blue eyes sparkling. Of course, I have no idea what he'll look like now! He might have a beard and his hair might be an unruly, unwashed mop, but I'll know Calum by his eyes - eyes that show such deep tenderness and love.

Dec. 31st

I don't know what to write today! My nerves are sending butterflies to my stomach! My mind is in a whirl! I can't believe it's actually happening, but my Calum IS coming home! Catriona's dress is finished and ironed, and I'm dreaming about meeting him. I can just imagine the scene. He'll come down the gangway - eyes searching the sea of faces for his wife - and I'll push forward with Catriona and be met by his warm embrace, and we'll never be separated again! Oh! I must try to sleep. It sounds as if the wind is rising, which won't help me.

Jan. 1st

I don't think I've ever been so afraid. It's two o'clock in the morning and the wind is roaring and screaming at the window. The rain is just pouring down and the waves are crashing onto the shore. I cannot sleep. All I can think of is Calum on that boat. Oh! I hope and pray that he will be all right and soon be home here by my side.

It is evening

I ran to the shore leaving Catriona asleep in her bed. With panic rising in my heart I searched sorrowfully amongst the bodies and débris on the shore line, stumbling across the stooped figures of mourning women who had already found their loved one. Bodies had been thrown up all over the shore, yet I couldn't see Calum, and there was still a flicker of hope in my heart. But then, I found him. . .

. . . His blue eyes, once filled with love and joy, were now lifeless, staring above me to the dark, grey sky. They were not the searching, smiling eyes I had yearned for so long to see. Just cold and vacant now, seeing nothing. I fell down beside him, sobbing out all my feelings, my heart broken. I touched him and he was cold. Seaweed was wrapped around his neck and sand covered his body, the lovely blond hair now wet and limp, his hands so cold in mine. I sat there for a long time, so overcome with grief that I didn't know what to do or think, deaf to all the hubbub around me. . .

A man from the village touched me gently on the shoulder and I knew they had come to take Calum away. Slowly, I leant over and kissed his cold, blue lips for the last time.

Catriona's green dress is folded away into a drawer. She will wear it someday, but she will not need it for the homecoming.

ISABEL STONE

THURSO HIGH SCHOOL

SECOND PRIZE, 1997/98

A Gulp of the Sahara

Nothing can be more frustrating than to be given a free choice for the topic of your composition. What a pain it is to try and think what to tell this world about. For indeed, can the world really be interested in how you were busy having your chickenpox? Helped your sister to 'drill' her piano exercises? Or went to visit your granny? Hardly likely! And my life experience mainly consists of such minor routine things, which are Everyday Life. But sometimes . . .

In Russia there is an old revolutionary song containing the following lines in it.

> *When bound for Odessa*
> *He brought us to Kherson. . .*

The song is about Sailor Zheleznyak who became infamous for the accuracy of his pilotage. And still he's nothing compared to my Mum. One day she went to buy air tickets for Simferopol, in the Ukraine, only to bring home two tourist vouchers to. . . Sousse, Tunisia. The way it happened was as follows. . . The independent spirit of our ex-compatriots had gone up so high that an air fare to Africa became much cheaper than the one to the Ukraine! There are no words to describe how warmly I welcomed this unscientific caprice of our transitory economy.

My relatives who had lived major parts of their lives behind the 'iron curtain' were filled with fright. . . My 97-year-old Great-Grandma Marousya asked me in an unusually trembling voice, "Tunisia? Where is it, grandson?" "The northern coast of Africa!" - was my proud reply. "The northern coast?" She sounded full of care and concern, "Won't you be cold there?". . .

So, the whirl of travelling (modestly and somewhat shabbily materialised in the image of a TU-154B jet belonging to the least indulgent service-provider in the world - Aeroflot) sweeps me high up into some unexperienced world. For a moment it seems to me that I have entered some virtual reality or climbed into the 'TV Travellers' Club' programme; from my window I can see far below the sloping humps of the Tatra Mountains, the aggressive, snow-covered peaks of the Alps, the 'boot' of Italy, the Mediterranean sea, Sicily . . . But here my thoughts are brought down to earth by our far-from-virtual air hostess: "What's that island over there?" she's asked. "Some island, there are many in this sea."

And so, for the first time in my life I find myself beyond Europe . . . We step out of the jet to dive into almost liquid heat. Palms, blond people, lace-like letters, sand, white cubes of houses, monotonously howling music, endless numbers of olive trees . . . and a whole new world of sensations.

Having soaked well in the very salty sea and charred our bodies under the very hot sun, we decided to partake of adventure and started out for a two-day safari. (In fact something surprising was happening to my vocabulary there in Tunisia. Some words like *safari*, *medina*, *souk*, *palms*, *oasis*, etc, had been familiar from books before, but there and then I experienced them, 'I lived them through'.
And the Magic Kaleidoscope began.

El-Jem . . . The ruins of an ancient Roman amphitheatre with ghosts of gladiators, proud invincible Berbers and early Christians tortured to death. . .

The Small Atlas Mountains . . . Unapproachable wall along the road. Mountains, sands, tiny patches of furry greenery and viscous air - not surprising that American film-makers once chose this place to shoot their *Star Wars*: on our planet they could not have found a more 'unearthly' landscape . . .

Matmata . . . The invisible Berber town with people living in dug-out caves up to now (only recently there appeared satellite aerials sticking out next to almost every dwelling). . .

El-Hamma . . . Hot springs of water amidst an oasis of date palms.

And **Douz** at last, **The Gate of the Sahara**. The end of familiar green life.

Muslims have a legend in which the Sahara originated in a garden arranged by Allah himself, from which he chose to abolish all life and vanity, to have a solitary place for contemplation.

Mortals feel uncomfortable there at first: small flurries of sand

everywhere make it difficult to breathe or move . . . Then we were mounted on camel backs and our caravan, loaded with clumsy European bodies, proceeded into the sands of the Sahara to drink in the view of the sunset. Some time passed before I caught the rhythm of that tall and very proud animal, made sense of it with all my kinaesthetic thinking and suddenly felt free.

One more word became internalized – the word *horizon*. I live in a big city in which wherever you look your eye comes across a house, a tree, a fence, a palace, a grille or a monument; there is no vastness there – your inner space being squeezed between the walls and boundaries. But in the Sahara my city resident's compressed inner space suddenly came out, meeting no hindrance on its way. My soul unfolded into something enormous and endless and I experienced some kind of elevation, and that felt great. In 45 minutes we stopped to watch the sunset – one of the celestial performances about changes and transitions. . .

A shrill unpleasant voice brought me down to earth (there was no telling the sex of this voice, for we were all wrapped up to the eyes in similar local gowns and *sheshes* (scarves). The voice demanded to be reimbursed for disappointment. "We've paid our money to be shown a landscape, but there's nothing but sand here."

The sun had set and we headed for the village whose name sounds like a line from the Arabian song - **El-Faouar**.

The way back lay through the *chottes* - the deadest deserts in the world with only the salty plain, the sky, and the perfectly-straight line of the horizon; the place where man reconsiders his self-esteem.

Tozeur ... **Carthage** ... **Tunis** ... **Sidi Bou Said** - a biblical looking town ... There was my way back home - the pleasure to which nothing compares, but this time I was coming home with the song of the Sahara in my heart - a song to a different kind of life that makes Man feel free and fall in love with the challenge. And it is this song that I have tried to share in my humble words:

> *In the sands of the Desert*
> *My soul, full of wisdom and freedom,*
> *Spent a dozen of hours which felt overwhelmingly short . . .*

DMITRI REVA

GYMNASIUM 272, ST PETERSBURG

FIRST PRIZE, 1996/97

Pigs Might Fly

Everybody says to me "Pigs might fly"
"Could you lend me a fiver?"
"Pigs might fly"
"Can I stay up till twelve?"
"And pigs might fly!"
The other day
I saw a pig with golden wings.
It soared across the sky,
Behind a cloud and then,
Hovering gracefully, it joined its companions,
And flew South for the winter.

HOLLY ARDEN

JAMES GILLESPIE'S HIGH SCHOOL

EDINBURGH

FIRST PRIZE, 1992/93

Russians in Scotland

Each year in May, at the time of the Pushkin Prizegiving, the Russian prizewinners are invited to spend a week in Scotland. In 1998 Daria (Dasha) Belova and Julia Gromova were our guests. The programme for their visit was arranged by Valerie Bierman, whose husband Michael kindly acted as principal chauffeur. Between them, and with help from others, the girls had a wonderful time, as can be seen from the account below, which is a compilation of the letters they sent to Valerie after their return home.

*D*asha *writes:* As a beautiful bracelet made of different and bright beads, this travel to Scotland consists of many glorious moments, adventures, feelings, the Pushkin Prizes presented to us. I cannot find the right words to explain our gratitude, so I'll simply say THANK YOU!

I am really thankful to the Pushkin Prizes and Lady Butter, especially for the help given to the beginners in the literature world, for the opportunity each year for some of them to visit Scotland, not as a tourist just trying to take as many pictures as possible, but to admire the real life of the people, to know more about the Scottish culture and traditions, and even to get acquainted with the young Scottish writers!.

Each day of our stay was full of too many outstanding things to remember. I think this would not have been so if it had not been for you and Michael. You were so kind and patient to be with us almost the whole time of our visit. *Julia writes:* We were always surrounded by people who took care of us and who were really interested in our having a good time. I remember well the evening we spent with Irene Dunlop and her husband. We talked about different things, mixing the two languages, English and Russian, because both of them know Russian very well. Later, at the Prizegiving, we met a lot of people from the older generation who studied Russian at school, and we were a bit surprised because we never thought this language could be studied in Scotland.

We spent a day in Glasgow, *writes Dasha*, where time ran too fast to see everything, but with the help of Kathryn and her wonderful friend we managed to visit the Modern Art Gallery. *Julia goes on:* It cannot be compared to anything, it was so great. There is no museum of such kind in St Petersburg. Dasha and I didn't want to leave it, so interesting were all the works of art.

Another curious thing we saw in Glasgow, with Mary, was a Russian opera, **The Queen of Spades**, sung in Russian by non-Russian singers. It made a great impression on both of us. *Dasha adds:* The voices were splendid, though certainly in some tragic and dramatic places it was great to hear - the Scottish accent!

On the train back they talked over all the events in Glasgow, 'which turned out to be very different from quiet, blossoming Edinburgh'.

And another charming evening, *Dasha continues*, when we first heard the music of the bagpipers, was given to us by Hannah (one of the last year's prizewinners) and her family. The food was delicious and the whole evening was very kind and lovely. I can't help smiling now when I think of it.

We were both impressed by the number of activities for the students at Broughton High School, *said Julia*. It's not usual for our schools to pay so much attention to creative activities, and there we saw wonderful art and design classes, theatre, books of stories written by children and published in the school magazine. It is no wonder that a creative competition like the Pushkin Prizes is organised in Scotland.

They also visited Biggar High School, where they sat in on an English lesson, and had a trip to Traquair House and St Mary's Loch.

Dasha ends: Before I thought of sending my poems for the Pushkin Prizes, I heard a woman on TV saying: 'Always try to give and someone will take it'. After our visit to Scotland, and getting acquainted with you and all the other people we met, I think this is a great motto to live by. And finally, I'd like to quote from Oscar Wilde's *The Ideal Husband:* 'An acquaintance that begins with a compliment is sure to develop into a real friendship'. If, supposing this prize given to me was a compliment from the Pushkin Prizes to my work, then our friendship is not a lost thing.

Scots in St Petersburg

Roddy Wallace's account of his visit to St Petersburg is representative of all the other reports written after the prizewinners' return.

Russia - in my mind a land of finger freezing weather and Lada ridden roads. Before the 21st September my sole impression of Russia was from the James Bond film *From Russia With Love* - that of turned up collars and furry hats to keep out the cold.

I had not counted on a cultural city, full of wonderful architecture and colour. The dour looking people in the film were, in fact, full of warmth and smiles. The previously suspicious sounding food (things like pumpkin porridge) turned out to be both tasty and filling (unlike Britain, every meal was made with fresh produce). The writing, that before seemed like some obscure code, was remarkably easy to make sense of, once you got the hang of it.

The reason I was in St Petersburg was because of Alexander Pushkin, the great Russian poet. One of the most interesting days of the trip was spent in Tsarskoje Selo (otherwise known as Pushkin) where Pushkin boarded and studied. . . You got a feel of just how talented he and his classmates were. Surprisingly, Pushkin's grades were not perfect, which shows how strict the teachers must have been. We looked at his timetables – lessons starting at 8 o'clock in the morning - and I realised how impossible life would be for bed-lovers like myself.

The highlight of my trip was visiting the three schools. A number of aspects about them amazed me - the one that struck me first was their resourcefulness. During the lovely concerts they put on, the enthusiasm shone out and afterwards, talking to the pupils, their astounding knowledge of English made me feel embarrassingly inadequate (one boy, when talking about how strange the English language was, told me that there were 'something like 16 tenses in English', a fact that I had to admit to him that I did not know).

Apart from their aptitude for foreign languages the other main difference between Russian and Scottish children is the pride Russian children hold for their schools. Countless pupils freely admitted how proud they were of their school - where I come from I think you'd be hard pushed to find one such student.

The historical side of the trip came from the palaces and museums we visited, each with different style or attraction. My favourite was the world famous Hermitage, more specifically the Impressionist floor. Cézanne, van Gogh, Renoir, Degas and Monet all had collections there. Other painters included Picasso, Matisse, Rembrandt and da Vinci. It was overwhelming to think that you were standing feet, sometimes inches, away from priceless works of art.

Thinking back I realise how much I enjoyed Russia. I think my lasting impression will be of the people. Natalya was the name of our wonderful hostess. She was small and cuddly and always had a smile on her face. Her English was good, but she spoke with a strong Russian accent which I liked - it sounded so natural, not as if she was trying to sound like someone she wasn't.

In stark contrast, Elena, our excellent guide, spoke English like a native. She was always very well dressed and wore her grey hair up in a bun. The style of her guided tours was perfect. She cut out any boring bits, dismissing them with a funny 'blah, blah, blah, la, la, la'. "Ah, my DALEENGS!" (Ah my darlings) she beamed, every time she greeted us. But of all the people we met, the biggest character was the father of Bogdan (the Russian prizewinner). He was a big, stout man and was multi-talented. He was a children's writer and a folk singer as well as being the leader of the area's Cossacks. He was upright and proud and I found him very amusing. You could call him a stereotype Russian - every time he threw back a shot of vodka it would be greeted by the routine of his young daughter holding a slice of ham which he would sniff, cross his eyes, and then take in air through his nostrils while shaking his bearded chops. I couldn't stop myself laughing.

On the morning of the day we returned we visited a Russian Orthodox Church. This was the only place where I felt unwelcome. As we lit a candle under the eyes of the saints (to grant us a safe journey back) my candle refused to light. In the end some hot wax landed on my hand. Was it a coincidence that, on the plane flight back, I was horribly and violently sick . . . ?

Other Impressions

'It (the whole experience) was the highlight of my teenage years'.

'The streets were all very wide, very long and very straight, quite different from Edinburgh. There didn't seem to be any shops, just little kiosks at the side of the road. It was Saturday, so many people had gone to their *dachas* in the country for the harvest'.

'Breakfast was a fish with sauce and a drink (cranberries and sugar) as well as *pirog* - cabbage pie'.

'What was surprising to me was the juxtaposition of all the grand palaces and the Russian people living in privation'.

'I noticed how proud Russian children are of their country and school. Education seems to be very important to them'.

'Although they do not live in such luxury as we do, I was deeply touched by how hospitable our hosts were'.

At the Hermitage Museum: 'We were amazed to learn that if we stopped to look at everything for two minutes it would take us NINE YEARS to get round!'

'I came away having acquired quite a taste for beetroot soup (*borscht*).'

At the Palace of Catherine the Great: 'Of all the buildings we saw, this was the most stunning. Splendid and picturesque it stood, its gold-covered sculptures and domes glistening in the sunshine. It was painted blue and white, like many St Petersburg palaces of that period. Inside, gold seemed to be everywhere, and the finest marble on the floor. Everyone entering has to put on large slippers over their shoes. Brilliant and ornate carvings decorated all the rooms. There was an amazing ballroom decorated entirely in gold leaf, and huge mirrors on the walls. In most rooms there were pictures of it after the German bombings, and the amount of restoration that had been done was truly unbelievable'.

'I did enjoy the dish of fried egg with diced ham in it, placed on a hollowed out piece of toast'.

These words from Hannah Bardell speak for all the prizewinners:
Looking back now, I realise how lucky I am to have had this experience, it is something I shall never forget as long as I live, it has given me so much. I have had the experience of a new country, culture and type of people, I have made many new friends, but to my mind the most important thing I have gained is a new outlook on life. It seems to me we all have a lot to learn from each other and our different ways of life.

Lastly, I would like to say how proud I was to go to Russia representing the Pushkin Prizes, and how grateful I am to everyone involved in the organisation for giving me this wonderful opportunity.

Давно
прошедшие года

Забуду ль давние года
И дружбу прежних дней?
Нет, не забуду никогда,
Поверь, мой друг, поверь.

Нальем мы красного вина
За старую любовь
И выпьем весь бокал до дна,
Чтоб встретиться нам вновь.

И вот моя рука, друг мой,
И дай свою ты мне,
Вино мы выпьем за любовь,
За дружбу прежних дней!

Translated by
Svetlana Morozkina
School No. 272,
St Petersburg

Auld Lang Syne

Should auld acquaintance be forgot
And never brought to mind?
Should auld acquaintance be forgot
And auld old lang syne!

And surely ye'll be your pint stowp!
And surely I'll be mine!
And we'll tak a cup o' kindness yet
For auld lang syne.

And there's hand, my trusty fere!
And gie's a hand o' thine!
And we'll tak a right gude-willie waught
For auld lang syne.

Chorus (not translated)
For auld lang syne, my dear,
For auld lang syne,
We'll tak a cup o' kindness yet
For auld lang syne